The Yoke of Jesus

If His yoke is easy, Why can life be so difficult?

Jesus said,
"Come to me, all you who are
weary and burdened, and I will give you rest…
For my yoke is easy and **my burden is light**."

(Matthew 11:28-30, NIV)

Really?
An easy yoke?
Have you seen my life?
And Jesus still wants to help others through me?

Rick Mills DVM, PhD, LMSW

http://TheYokeOfJesus.com

Version 1.00

Cover photo: Randi by Rick Mills

Cover artwork: Rick, Georgeann, Becca, and Bonnie Mills
Interior layout: Rick, Georgeann, Becca, Bonnie, and Makayla Mills

ISBN: 978-0-9862236-4-8

RF Publishing
Ames, IA 50014

We are born into a difficult world of deceiving lies, and redeemed into Jesus' body of renewing love.

Randi

Contents

PREFACE

This is not a happy happy yippee yippee God is good and here's the combination for your life-to-be-great book. Notice the part in the title that says, "Why can life be so difficult?" As such, it is not my goal to reinforce naïveté and build false hope. Rather, it is to build wisdom and true hope founded in Jesus who explained to His disciples, "I have told you these things, so that in me you may have peace. In this world you will have trouble. But take heart! I have overcome the world" (John 16:33). If this is true, it is only when we are *false hopeless* that we can place our true hope in Him.

Some difficulties in life are unavoidable and are inflicted on us through the free will that God gives others and ourselves. That acknowledged, there are also many difficulties that can be avoided with wisdom and a similar exercise of our free will. Since we are on this journey through life together, when it comes to the difficulties we encounter, God wants us to praise Him, have peace in His Son Jesus, become wise, and teach others to do the same. This book is my effort to help you and me take a faithful step in that direction.

As part of my desire to continue with you on your journey, I have created a companion website to this book, http://TheYokeOfJesus.com, where I will periodically offer additional thoughts based on my own personal growth, and comments from you and others. If you have insights or helpful suggestions that you would like to share with me, I would love to hear from you.

ACKNOWLEDGEMENTS

Thank you brothers of Iowa Quest. Each year we meet and wait week after week after week to hear what God has been doing in our lives that the Holy Spirit then uses to form in us what the Quest weekend will cover. I have never been associated with a group of men more passionate, committed, and submitted to one another as unto the Lord. I was praying with you on January 19, 2013 when I received the inspiration for this book. And for the life of me I cannot remember who came up with the idea of "one mores," but I can assure you that a Quest weekend with you will always be a *one more* of mine.

I deeply appreciate Gary and Elaine Roys, and Walter Hearn, who faithfully suffered through an early draft of this book.

Thank you, Ann Smiley-Oyen. You are a master of the big picture and in moving sections of the book to where they belonged. Two thoughts of yours stand out in my mind, "Hey, that's a great ending, it really should be in the middle," and, "By the way, do you know you have two books here?" Ann, your commitment to excellence is unwavering and inspiring.

Thank you, Paul Smiley-Oyen, for your tutorial on fonts and strokes and X heights and a whole lot more that I have forgotten. I hope I have not strayed too far from your advice.

Thank you, Terry and Sue Castor, for your enduring friendship over many years. Terry, your comments on the manuscript came from a truly unique and always insightful perspective. You have an amazing eye for detail, meaning, and flow.

Thank you, Rick and Karen Orozco, for the grace and joy I have experienced from you beginning in our first Bible study together with Terry and Sue in 1975. Rick, you have always been a source of encouragement and hope. My father-in-law used to say on a hot summer day, "Be patient, God will send a cool breeze." Your telephone call to me after you read a draft of this book was that breeze.

Thank you to my Mother, Mary L. Martin, for your tireless efforts at reading multiple drafts of this book. I will always remember with fondness the hours upon hours that we were on the phone together choosing among words and deciding on punctuation. I have benefited immeasurably from your commitment to education, which began when you were a child sitting next to a kerosene lamp.

Thank you to my daughters, Becca and Bonnie, who have always been a blessing to Georgeann and me. Your tenacity has occasionally been an inconvenient virtue, especially when I thought I was finished formatting the cover and layout of this book. Both of you have convinced me with your patient and loving persistence that a pixel here and there, and a one half font size difference can translate into a feeling of "Yeah! That's it!"

Consistent with "the first shall be last," I am so completely grateful to my wife, Georgeann.

You read this book numerous times beginning well before it was even qualified to be called a first draft. More importantly, for over forty years we have learned and lived what is in this book together without knowing there would even be a book. Your commitment to loving Jesus and listening to the Holy Spirit have provided light to me in the midst of darkness more often than I can count. I especially appreciate your notes in the margins such as, "Powerful," "Heavy," "Deep," and "I still don't like this paragraph!"

I cannot imagine my journey through life without you.

DEDICATION

This book is dedicated to those who are seeking Jesus and trying to be His feet, arms, and hands to others in need before a watching world. May you grow in wisdom and perseverance on your journey. You matter, and the difference you make in the lives of others matters.

INTRODUCTION

---

28 "Come to me, all you who are weary and burdened, and I will give you rest. 29 Take my yoke upon you and learn from me, for I am gentle and humble in heart, and you will find rest for your souls. 30 For my yoke is easy and my burden is light." (Matthew 11:28-30)

If Jesus is who He says He is in the Bible, there is no decision more important than accepting His invitation to come to Him and take His yoke upon you. He claims that once you do, you can learn from Him and find rest for your soul. But what does His yoke look like? What does it feel like? And for that matter, what kind of relationship requires a yoke?

The Bible is full of illustrations to help us understand our relationship with Jesus. Obviously, none is singularly sufficient or there would not be so many. Each, however, reveals a portion of truth that when combined with others moves us closer to understanding our relationship with Him.

In this book I use the illustration of an ox cart to help you examine your relationship with Jesus, with others, and with yourself. I explore your oneness and separateness in Him along with what it means to wear His yoke. I also describe the often stark contrast between who others may say you are with whom God declares you to be. I also identify many difficulties you may encounter in your life, and God's provision for overcoming them.

Since part of God's provision is His Son's body, the Church, I will compare a healthy congregation to a Club of christ (lowercase "c" intended). I will also offer insight into strategies for helping others in a way that does not compromise your own physical, mental, emotional, and spiritual well-being. Most of these insights come from Scripture, while others are based in biblical counseling.

This book describes a wide range of personal experiences that for some will be unpleasant to read, and for others, painful to remember. It may even be that for you, your own circumstances and experiences are even worse. My purpose is not to open old wounds unnecessarily, but rather, to shed light on any existing wounds that continue to cause you difficulty by influencing your current thoughts, decisions, and actions. Hopefully, this light will bring clarity, though unfortunately, clarity often comes with its own pain and difficulty.

While you can benefit greatly from reading this book on your own, I encourage you to read it with at least one other Christian so that together, you can pray and work through the questions in each chapter. It is often in the eyes of a trusted brother or sister that God's truth, and the truth of our past experiences are reflected more accurately than what we can perceive on our own. That said, no brother or sister is perfect, and anything you receive into your thinking must first be in alignment with Scripture, and also be consistent with your discernment from the Holy Spirit.

If reading this book triggers strong and overwhelming emotions from your past or current circumstances, please take a break from reading, put yourself first, and talk with a qualified counselor, pastor, family member, or a supportive friend. This may be *your time* to courageously reach out for help.

I caution you against three common reactions while reading this book. The first is a tendency to minimize your past and current difficulties by comparing them to someone else who "has it worse." Your difficulties do not become less important or less painful just because someone else "has it worse." If Jesus thought this, He would only have died for the "worst" sinner in the world.

The second caution is that the beginning chapters identify difficulties originating early in life from parents or caregivers, which includes grandparents, relatives, adoptive parents, stepparents, step-grandparents, step-relatives, childcare workers, teachers, coaches, and anyone else who has a direct influence on a person's development during his or her formative years. Often, our love for these people can cause us to minimize and rationalize their painful actions. You might do this by thinking, "They did the best they could," or "They didn't mean to cause me harm." I understand your desire to protect their image in your mind, and perhaps even their own image in their own mind, but think about a situation in which a six-year-old child in a parked car with the engine running, accidentally bumps the gear shift into reverse. He then tries his best to steer the moving car as it knocks you down and rolls over your leg that is now broken. Hearing from bystanders that "He tried his best," or "He didn't mean to hurt you," does not make your leg any less broken or less painful. You are still left with the reality of restoring your leg so you will not walk with a limp, or run from all cars that appear to be carrying a six-year-old child.

The third caution is to not waste your precious time and energy bitterly judging your parents or caregivers, or anyone else who has harmed you, because to do so not only lengthens and deepens your wounds, it also robs you of yet another day of your life. While anger and judging others can produce feelings of superiority, power, and control, which are more personally tolerable than those of vulnerability, sadness, and fear, they are not a comfortable yoke and do not provide rest for your soul.

As for parents and caregivers in general, the majority do not wake up each morning asking themselves, "How can I mess this kid up even more today?" It is more likely that they cannot give what they never received and do not have. If that is your experience, it is now up to you to find healing and renewal so you can reclaim God's intended life for you and those you love.

While we are commanded not to judge others, when we have a difficult experience with someone, there is nothing wrong with making a clear assessment of what happened, and wisely taking steps to prevent it from happening again. For example, after your leg was healed from the six-year-old's best effort at steering a car, if you once again find yourself walking behind a parked car with its engine running, it would be prudent to be alert whether it contained a six-year-old child or not. On the other hand, if after your leg is physically healed you refuse to walk near any parked car, engine running or not, and hate or fear all children, you still have some mental and emotional wounds that need healing before you can once again walk in freedom with wisdom.

Life *can be* difficult because life *is* difficult. When the Apostle Paul asks, "Who shall separate us from the love of Christ? Shall trouble or hardship or persecution or famine or nakedness or danger or sword?" (Romans 8:35), he is referring to some serious difficulties. He answers his question beginning with verse 37,

> [37] No, in all these things we are more than conquerors through him who loved us. [38] For I am convinced that neither death nor life, neither angels nor demons, neither the present nor the future, nor any powers, [39] neither height nor depth, nor anything else in all creation, will be able to separate us from the love of God that is in Christ Jesus our Lord. (Romans 8:37-39)

If as Paul writes, we are "more than conquerors," then evidently we are in a war, and that war started long before any of us were born, and will continue until Jesus returns. In the meantime, the best we can hope for is to enter into a oneness relationship with Him and His body of believers; grow in our knowledge, understanding, and wisdom; and live an abundant life in the midst of our difficulties through the power of the Holy Spirit.

Any understanding you or I can have about God is by definition incomplete because He said, "As the heavens are higher than the earth, so are my ways higher than your ways and my thoughts than your thoughts" (Isaiah 55:9). With this in mind, I fully accept and even proclaim that the ox cart is yet another singularly insufficient illustration of our relationship with Jesus, and I do not offer it as a *lost book* of the Bible. As such, please do not push this cart beyond where I leave it.

The overall message of this book is that we are born into a difficult world of deceiving lies, and *can be* redeemed into Jesus' body of renewing love. You have a choice. Everyone wears a yoke, and your choice of whose you wear will determine to what extent you live your life abundantly. If you take the yoke of Jesus and learn from Him, God will use your painful and difficult experiences along with His healing grace to renew and conform you to the image of His Son.

I hope this ox cart illustration and the Chapters on helping others will be used by the Holy Spirit to deepen your understanding of God's truth, and bring about in you a greater oneness with Jesus, with others, and within yourself; it has for me.

SECTION 1

Wearing a Yoke

———————

CHAPTER 1

Yokes

The purpose of a yoke is to help an animal such as an ox pull a cart more effectively. An ideal yoke is strong, light, and fits comfortably as it evenly distributes around the neck and shoulders the pressure of pulling a load. A heavy and ill-fitting yoke makes pulling any load much more difficult than need be.

In Matthew 11, Jesus spoke to His potential followers about His yoke when He said:

> 28 "Come to me, all you who are weary and burdened, and I will give you rest. 29 Take my yoke upon you and learn from me, for I am gentle and humble in heart, and you will find rest for your souls. 30 For my yoke is easy and my burden is light." (Matthew 11:28-30)

If Jesus offers a yoke that is easy, what can that yoke be? A key to understanding His easy yoke may be found in the apparent contrast between His yoke and that of the religious leaders at that time.

The Yoke of the Religious Leaders

The idea of a yoke being worn by followers of a religious leader was familiar to Jesus' listeners, and it implied that followers would join and become a replica of their leader. From Jesus' offer, it is clear that His listeners were weary and burdened, and they needed rest. When He said, "learn from me" and that He was "gentle and humble in heart," the implication is that His listeners had already learned laws and rules from their demanding religious leaders who were neither gentle nor humble. It is also apparent that the yoke of the religious leaders did not provide rest for their souls, and in fact made their lives even more difficult and burdensome.

It is also likely that the yoke of the religious leaders did not meet the needs of the poor and the outcast. Perhaps the laws and customs were originally implemented to bring about spiritual maturity and to honor God, but evolved gradually into a religious system of control and manipulation that served the needs and desires of the religious leaders rather than easing the burdens of their followers. Either way, Jesus was so *impressed* by the yoke of the religious leaders and the replication of their lives in their followers that He said later in Matthew 23,

> "Woe to you, teachers of the law and Pharisees, you hypocrites! You travel over land and sea to win a single convert, and when you have succeeded, you make them twice as much a child of hell as you are." (Matthew 23:15)

Jesus is not offering an *easier* and *lighter* religion. To the contrary, based on what He said about adultery in Matthew Chapter 5, He raises the bar of performance standards for righteousness even higher.

> "But I tell you that anyone who looks at a woman lustfully has already committed adultery with her in his heart." (Matthew 5:28)

You can be born into a religious yoke, but you cannot be born into Jesus' yoke. He says, "Come to me" and "Take my yoke upon you." This is an intentional act of your will to come to Him and receive from Him. He did not say, "I will chase you down and strap this thing around your neck." Jesus expects wearied and burdened people to come to Him with any yokes they are currently wearing, and take His.

Removing a Yoke

Removing a yoke and exchanging it for the yoke of Jesus is not easy. When I was a practicing veterinarian, a client brought me her half-shaved dog from the groomer. Every spring he would get his "lion cut" that left a full mane on his head and a small tuft on the end of his tail. The justification for this stylish makeover was that he would be cool in the summer. From a temperature perspective he was definitely cooler, however, from a dog's perspective when he saw his friends at the park, I'm not sure he or they would say he looked all that cool.

The reason for his visit was that several months earlier someone had placed a rubber band around his neck, and it had gone unnoticed until it was discovered by the groomer. Sections of it had cut into his neck and there were areas where the skin had healed over with significant scarring. The owner was shocked that it was there because she had not noticed him having any discomfort. I anesthetized him, reopened the scarred areas, removed the rubber band, and sutured his wounds.

Religious, cultural, social, and family yokes can be a lot like that rubber band. They get put on our neck without our consent, are difficult to remove, and we eventually get used to them along with any discomfort they cause. Unfortunately, when it comes to removing these yokes there is no anesthesia for the surgery.

[Side note: While the dog was waking up from anesthesia, a high school student who had just arrived to observe for the afternoon was stunned to see what appeared to be a continuous line of sutures around the dog's neck. My explanation that I had successfully completed a head transplant was rudely interrupted when my assistant returned and gave assurances to the contrary.]

Questions

1) Have you ever worn a difficult and heavy yoke that was placed on you by someone else? If so, what made it difficult and heavy?

2) If Jesus offers an easier yoke and a lighter burden, what does "easy" and "light" mean to you?

3) Were you born into any yokes that are in conflict with what Jesus is offering? If so, are they still on your neck? Are you experiencing any shortness of breath? What scars have they left?

Oneness and Separateness in Our Relationship With Jesus

While the religious leaders expected their followers to join them and become replicas, Jesus wants a different kind of relationship with us. Some illustrations in the Bible portray this relationship from a *separateness* perspective as between two separate individuals, while others emphasize a *oneness* perspective.

Our separateness in our relationship with Jesus is portrayed in the following illustration from the book of Revelation where He says,

> "Here I am! I stand at the door and knock. If anyone hears my voice and opens the door, I will come in and eat with that person, and they with me." (Revelation 3:20)

This passage is written about a believer, and reflects a sense of individual separateness in our relationship with Jesus because we must respond to His knock and intentionally open the door in order for Him to *come in* and *eat with* us.

A passage that describes both our intimate separateness and oneness with Jesus is found in John Chapter 15 where Jesus is talking with His disciples and says,

> "I am the vine; you are the branches. If you remain in me and I in you, you will bear much fruit; apart from me you can do nothing." (John 15:5)

Jesus plainly states that He is the vine and we are connected to Him as branches. This illustration emphasizes our separateness because we are not the vine, nor is He our branch. On the other hand, when He talks about us remaining in Him and Him remaining in us, that is about as *oneness* as it gets. On top of that when He says, "apart from me you can do nothing," from a spiritual perspective we are *functionally one* with Him as well.

Our oneness in our relationship with God and the importance of our life to Him are described in 1 John.

> [9] This is how God showed his love among us: He sent his one and only Son into the world that we might live

through him. [10] This is love: not that we loved God, but that he loved us and sent his Son as an atoning sacrifice for our sins. [11] Dear friends, since God so loved us, we also ought to love one another. [12] No one has ever seen God; but if we love one another, God lives in us and his love is made complete in us.

[13] This is how we know that we live in him and he in us: He has given us of his Spirit. [14] And we have seen and testify that the Father has sent his Son to be the Savior of the world. [15] If anyone acknowledges that Jesus is the Son of God, God lives in them and they in God. [16] And so we know and rely on the love God has for us. (1 John 4:9-16)

God first loved us by sending His Son "that we might live through Him." It was not our good works that motivated God, rather, it was our need and His love. God sent Jesus "as an atoning sacrifice for our sins," and what does He want in return? The answer is in verse 11, "Dear friends, since God so loved us, we also ought to love one another." Doesn't that seem a bit odd? Shouldn't it say "we also ought to *love God in return.*" No, in this passage John is saying that our response to God's love for us should be to love His other children. If you are a parent, this makes perfect sense. You no doubt appreciate it when someone helps you when you are in need, but how much more do you appreciate it when someone helps your child?

Our importance to God and His purpose for us is made clear in verse 12, which states, "No one has ever seen God; but if we love one another, God lives in us and his love is made complete in us." Not only is God willing to live in us, His love "is made complete in us." And then, as if we might still not understand our oneness in God, John writes verse 15, which presents the basis and truth of our oneness in a single sentence. "If anyone acknowledges that Jesus is the Son of God, God lives in them and they in God."

Is it not strange that our oneness with God results in Him living in us, yet our understanding cannot fully comprehend Him? This means that we are adequate enough to be His dwelling place and to be used by Him, yet inadequate when it comes to understanding Him fully. It seems that from God's perspective we are His *sufficiently inadequate* children. As we will see later, He also transforms those who accept His Son's sacrifice for their sins into a temple of the Holy Spirit.

Questions

1) What is your experience of oneness and separateness with Jesus?

2) Why would Jesus want to live His life through you, and how could that bring rest to your soul?

A Single Opening Yoke or a Double?

From a oneness and a separateness perspective, what do you *traditionally* picture in your mind when you think of Jesus' yoke? Do you envision a single yoke, which has an opening for one ox, or a double, which has openings for two? Matthew does not specify either, but several authors have proposed that Jesus was referring to a double yoke. One reason for this interpretation is that Jesus said, "learn from me," and one approach to training a young ox is to yoke it with another that is more experienced.

When interpreting His yoke as a double, there is a positive implication for *oneness* which is, we are not alone when yoked with Him because He is walking with us step by step. That said, there is a negative implication of separateness which is that Jesus has His side of the yoke and we have ours. There is also a performance implication of a double yoke which is that Jesus has His work to do on His side of the yoke, and we have our work to do on ours. I could more easily accept the interpretation of a double yoke if there was any indication that the religious leaders at that time were *equally* yoked with their weary and burdened followers.

While a double yoke has negative implications for separateness and performance, a single yoke seems to have even more. What could be more lonely and difficult than a single ox with a single yoke pulling a cart that contained a heavy load? If a double yoke is bad and a single is worse, what kind of yoke is Jesus offering? The answer lies nestled in the vine and branches of John Chapter 15. Let's read it again.

> "I am the vine; you are the branches. If you remain in
> me and I in you, you will bear much fruit; apart from
> me you can do nothing." (John 15:5)

Jesus Is the Yoke

I assert that Jesus was offering a very personal single yoke that is none other than Himself. I propose that His yoke can be seen as His arm around you that helps you pull your load and overcome the difficulties in your life as you *lean* into Him. From this perspective, everything Jesus says about His yoke makes perfect sense. *His arm is easy* and *the burden of His arm is light.* He does not add weight or difficulty to your life.

Seeing Jesus Himself as your personal yoke is consistent with the intimate relationship He describes of being united with Him as a branch is to its vine. It is from this intimacy that He makes all things possible, including learning from Him and finding rest for your soul. In addition, if His arm is around you, and His arm is around me, we are yoked together in His body and He is our head. Being united in Him enables us to help each other. So how many openings are in His yoke? One for each of His followers.

Questions

1) If Jesus is your yoke, what does that mean to you, and what do you think He should feel like?

2) Is it possible that the arm of Jesus could replace and heal you of the yokes that were placed on you by others? What about the yokes you willingly stepped into?

In the next chapter we will look at Jesus' disciples along with the mission he gave them because if anyone was expected to wear His *easy yoke* and carry His *light burden* it was they.

CHAPTER 2

His Disciples Wore His Yoke

Matthew Chapter 10 begins with Jesus sending His disciples out into the world and telling them what they would encounter.

Their Mission

The passage begins with a distinctly positive tone.

> 10:1 Jesus called his twelve disciples to him and gave them authority to drive out impure spirits and to heal every disease and sickness.
>
> 2 These are the names of the twelve apostles: first, Simon (who is called Peter) and his brother Andrew; James son of Zebedee, and his brother John; 3 Philip and Bartholomew; Thomas and Matthew the tax collector; James son of Alphaeus, and Thaddaeus; 4 Simon the Zealot and Judas Iscariot, who betrayed him.
>
> 5 These twelve Jesus sent out with the following instructions: "Do not go among the Gentiles or enter any town of the Samaritans. 6 Go rather to the lost sheep of Israel. 7 As you go, proclaim this message: 'The kingdom of heaven has come near.' 8 Heal the sick, raise the dead, cleanse those who have leprosy, drive out demons. Freely you have received; freely give." (Matthew 10:1-8)

Who would not want the authority to drive out impure spirits and demons, and the ability to heal every disease and sickness, raise the dead, and cleanse those who have leprosy? And for that matter, be part of a committed group that was doing the same. However, what follows in verses 9 and 10 may have caused His disciples some concern.

> [9] "Do not get any gold or silver or copper to take with you in your belts— [10] no bag for the journey or extra shirt or sandals or a staff, for the worker is worth his keep." (Matthew 10:9-10)

This sounds like being vulnerable and having trust are required. Then comes verses 16 and 17 with more instructions on how they are being sent out, along with how they will be received.

> [16] "I am sending you out like sheep among wolves. Therefore be as shrewd as snakes and as innocent as doves.

> [17] "Be on your guard; you will be handed over to the local councils and be flogged in the synagogues. [18] On my account you will be brought before governors and kings as witnesses to them and to the Gentiles. [19] But when they arrest you, do not worry about what to say or how to say it. At that time you will be given what to say, [20] for it will not be you speaking, but the Spirit of your Father speaking through you." (Matthew 10:16-20)

Jesus did not say they *might be* handed over to the local councils and flogged in the synagogues; He said they *would be*. And, it is clear from Matthew 11:28-30 that these difficult and heavy experiences would happen while they were wearing His *easy yoke* and carrying His *light burden*.

Chapters 10 and 11 of Matthew make it obvious that wearing Jesus' *easy yoke* does not mean a life without difficulties. To the contrary, life in many ways becomes even more difficult for those who take Jesus as their personal yoke.

Questions

1) If you were standing with the disciples when Jesus was speaking, do you think you would have gone with them or left? What concerns if any would you have had?

2) What concerns if any do you have today about being sent out as His disciple who is expected to wear His *easy* yoke and carry His *light* burden?

In the next section we will explore the ox cart illustration in greater detail. If Jesus is our yoke, the obvious conclusion is that we are the ox. But who is the driver and what is the cart? What do the wheels represent? What is the path we should follow? What about the other ox carts on our path, or other paths that cross our own? And why can life be so difficult?

SECTION 2

The Ox Cart

A brief overview of the oxcart illustration is as follows. The driver embodies our mind that consists of our thoughts, will, and emotions, and the ox corresponds to our body and physical strength. The cart represents our capabilities both natural and spiritual, and the wheels represent how we interact with others and our circumstances. The load in the cart is the ministry and responsibilities God has entrusted to us.

Each of these components of the ox cart illustration can be a source of difficulty that the easiest, lightest, and most comfortable yoke cannot prevent. And why should it? The purpose of Jesus' yoke is to help us fulfill our ministry and responsibilities, during which many difficulties cannot be avoided. Recall His promise to send His disciples out "like sheep among wolves," and that they would be taken before councils and flogged in the synagogues.

Being sent out like sheep, however, does not mean Christians are condemned to remain naïve. As Jesus said, we can learn from Him, and be "as shrewd as snakes" while remaining "as innocent as doves." God the Father, Jesus, the Holy Spirit, and wise parents, caregivers, friends, pastors, teachers, and counselors can teach us the wisdom we need to avoid many of life's difficulties. And for those difficulties that cannot be avoided, we can bring glory to God by enduring them with grace as "more than conquerors."

CHAPTER 3

The Driver

As comforting as the thought of Jesus being our personal yoke might be, He offers us much more. He offers a oneness that infuses, strengthens, and enables every part of our being with the Holy Spirit. As such, Jesus does not sit meekly on the back of our cart to be paraded before others. Neither does He sit mysteriously on a distant throne to be pleased by our frantic efforts to perform our way into His presence and approval. He has no desire to be like a parent at a playground whose child runs from one piece of equipment to another yelling, "Look at me, look at me. Did you see what I did? Look at me." Rather, He wants an intimate vine and branch relationship with each of us so He and we can say, "Look at us. Look at what we did together."

When I think of our relationship with God, I am reminded of a story about a man who cleaned up a vacant lot and turned it into a vegetable garden. One day he brought some of his vegetables to church and asked one of his friends, "Would you like some vegetables that I grew in my garden?" His friend took a slow all-knowing breath, which he exhaled even more slowly and asked, "Don't you mean God's garden?" The man paused, and took his own all-knowing breath and replied, "Well, I guess you're right, but you should have seen it when He owned it all by Himself."

When we first hear Jesus' invitation to take His yoke, we are like that vacant lot that we own all by ourselves. As we intentionally yield and respond to Him, He becomes our gardener who removes the debris, tills the soil, plants the seeds, and harvests His crop. Each of us is His unique garden that He cultivates to bring to the world the fruit of the Spirit it needs. It is also during this process that we grow in our relationship with Him, which is complicated by the fact that we are not a plot of stationary and choiceless ground. We choose to remain and respond – or not.

Returning to our separateness and oneness with God, and His working in and through us, Francis Chan, in his book, *Forgotten God: Reversing our Tragic Neglect of the Holy Spirit*, uses the term "both-ness" when referring to "God's action" and our "response-action." He cites Philippians,

> [12] Therefore, my dear friends, as you have always obeyed — not only in my presence, but now much more in my absence — continue to work out your salvation with fear and trembling, [13] for it is God who works in you to will and to act in order to fulfill his good purpose. (Philippians 2:12-13)

We are told to *work out* our salvation with God who *works in us to will and to act*. Both are required for us to live our lives in relationship with Him. As such, it matters which choices we make and what we do. Otherwise we are nothing more than thinking, feeling, and sometimes squealing puppets. I cannot imagine a God of the Universe having a desire to be a puppeteer with His hand in a limp sock. As to the question, "Is it me or is it God?", the complicated answer is, "Yes." It is just that simple and complex. Albert Einstein once said, "Everything should be made as simple as possible, but no simpler," which is especially true about our relationship with God.

For those who are uncomfortable with life's uncertain complexity and must conjure up a *mere feeling of certainty*, their answer is to blindly oversimplify matters with black or white thinking and then ignore what does not fit. I submit, however, that it is not an *overly simplistic blind faith* that pleases God. Rather, what pleases God is sighted faith that does not need to see through the mist of unknowns that often conceal our path. This faith is not covering our eyes, plugging our ears, and chanting

"Na-na-na-na-na, I am saved," though sometimes that may be the best we can do in the face of a severe difficulty. Faith that pleases God is looking directly into the face of uncertainty and life's difficulties, and believing the face of Jesus. This means that as limited as our God-ordained, incomplete understanding is, it is *adequate enough* for us to have a personal relationship with Jesus, and to respond to Him by choosing to live our lives in faith as branches of His vine.

Given the mystery that driving our cart emerges both from our *separateness* and *oneness in* Jesus, which is our connection to Him and belonging in Him, and from *our work* and *God working* in us, where did you and I get our thoughts that result in our decisions about what to believe about ourselves and how to drive our cart?

Learning to Drive Our Cart

You and I came into this world with a brain, but not much of a mind. We were naïve and helpless in every way, and we were not alone.

For better or for worse, all of us found ourselves with parents and caregivers who were not of our choosing. Many of these people had mental and emotional issues of varying degrees and, despite their age, were themselves frustrated and angry children on the inside. Their minds were complex and well-developed, though sometimes not developed well.

Many parents and caregivers also struggled with personal and relationship issues. They had agendas that we were either a part of, or from which we were a distraction. And to make matters even more complicated, we had a whole host of our own preprogrammed traits and tendencies just waiting to be triggered and expressed depending on our circumstances and our interactions with others.

Let Our Training Begin

Some children had reasonably good parents and caregivers who taught them that no one is all good or all bad. These children learned they had good traits and traits that were not-so-good. The not-so-good traits could be accepted without self-condemnation, and intentionally changed. They also learned that their lack of *perfection* in the eyes of others did not mean they were fundamentally bad, or would be ignored or even abandoned.

These children learned how to ask for help, and they received it without being ridiculed. They also learned that experiencing failure was an inevitable requirement for achieving success, and that no one is *perfect* at anything. These children learned that when they hurt someone, they could admit it, ask for forgiveness, and the relationship could be restored. Of course the reverse was also learned that when hurt by someone, they were taught how to handle their own strong emotions and to forgive that person even before he or she thought to ask for it. And if their offender did ask for forgiveness, these children learned how to forgive, and wisely reestablish the relationship with an appropriate level of trust.

The parents and caregivers of these children also taught them how to accept praise by giving them praise, and how to receive valid criticism without feeling condemned. These children also learned how to praise others, and to be content when others received praise. As such, these children learned how to not only enjoy being the center of attention, they also learned how to allow others to have the same.

These children also experienced a healthy separateness and oneness in their relationships with parents and caregivers. Separateness was experienced when they were encouraged to develop an independent sense of self by being allowed to explore their world and to become individually competent. Their right to have and express their own thoughts and emotions was respected and cultivated. Oneness was experienced through healthy family bonds and a sense of belonging that did not depend on performance. These children developed a stable mental and emotional foundation for managing the difficulties of life.

Unfortunately, God does not have enough wise and *sufficiently inadequate* parents to keep the planet populated, or enough well-balanced caregivers to help all children develop into healthy young adults. He has to do the best He can with those He has and provide for any difficult consequences that children experience.

For many children, and possibly you, childhood was very different from what I have just described. Some children were neglected and had to fend for themselves. Others were abused physically, mentally, emotionally, and/or sexually. Some were told they were stupid and weak and that they would never amount to anything, while others were told they were not worthy of being loved. Some children were even told they were so worthless they should not have been born. And on top of that, some went to school and received more of the same from their peers, and perhaps even from a frustrated teacher.

It is difficult for a child to fight back against such hostility. Parents and caregivers are too big and peers are too many. Each abusive blow that is not understood and released is absorbed and stored. Many children do not have someone in their life who can take them aside and ask, "Did you ever notice that people who call you stupid aren't all that bright?" No one is there to explain, "When people cannot accept their own flaws and shame, they often lash out at someone else – anyone else – and sometimes it just happens to be you."

Some children respond to rejection from their parents, caregivers, and others by trying even harder to win their approval, which can persist well into and perhaps throughout adulthood. These children often strive continually for an *unachievable perfection*. Unfortunately for many, even when they finally do hear words of affirmation from others later in life, these children have not learned how to receive them, let alone believe they are true. In fact, these affirmations can even be so much at odds with their own beliefs about themselves, the very sound of them can bring about feelings of discomfort, distress, or anxiety.

Some children learn there is no way to win the approval and acceptance of others so they *act out* their frustration, anger, and rage through defiant and destructive behaviors. Their logic, conscious or not, is summed up in the statement, "If you are going to reject me, you will at least do it on my terms." Sadly, this resolve brings about even more rejection, pain, and consequences.

Children who do not *act out* their frustration, anger, and rage often *focus it inward* resulting in self-loathing and despair. They take on both the role of abuser and the abused. They recall and replay the memorized and internalized accusations of their abusers with a slight and even more sinister mutation. They replace the word "You" with "I." They say to themselves, "I am stupid and weak. I will never be loved. I am so worthless I should never have been born." It is easy to understand why their inner voice is one of condemnation because it was built from the condemning voices of people around them. These children have succumbed to the dangerous habit of believing what they are told.

Questions

1) What was childhood like for you?

2) How reliable were your parents and childhood caregivers?

3) What lies, if any, do you believe about yourself based on your childhood experiences?

4) If people criticized and rejected you, is it possible they were wrong? Is it possible that God sees you differently?

5) What does praise from others feel like to you?

6) How often do you praise yourself when you have done something well? Do you always have to find a flaw? If so, why?

Childhood Agendas

A difficult childhood often causes young adults to emerge with various emotionally charged agendas to prevent further wounding and to satisfy their unmet needs. Unfortunately, these agendas can have unintended consequences.

For some young adults, the agenda is *control-based* with the mission of training everyone to give them what they want when they want it. Other young adults are stuck in childhood and want everyone to be the all-gratifying parents they never had. And when a *surrogate-adulthood-parent* fails to satisfy those perpetual longings for a happy childhood, which is impossible, he or she is met with the fury of an angry child in the body of a fully formed adult.

For other young adults the agenda is *approval-based*, which is a continuation of their efforts to please their parents, caregivers, and peers in order to be accepted. People with this agenda usually end up tired, disillusioned, and angry because others cannot provide enough *approval* to fill their childhood void and adulthood demands, or to overcome their inner disapproval of themselves.

The *approval-based agenda* can be pictured as someone standing in the middle of a circle of church and family members, friends, bosses, and coworkers with each calling out, "Over here, over here. Come over here and take care of this." And these shouts sound like whispers compared to the person's inner voice yelling, "Over there, over there. Get over there and take care of that. You are such a failure." People who are caught in the bondage of an approval-based agenda live in a whirlwind of frantic activity with the feeling that no one is pleased, including themselves.

The problem for those who always try to please others is the assumed contract that if they do everything others say they want, the reward will be love and acceptance. Unfortunately, pleasers eventually discover that those who do not love and accept them, always demand more, and will never welcome them into a meaningful relationship that provides contentment and rest for their soul. The only relationship that exists is one of disposable utility, not unlike a used paper plate or tissue, or a container of juice that is discarded when drained. The relationship that Jesus wants with you is nothing like this. If you find yourself discarded and drained, it was not His doing.

The agenda for other young adults is to reject their unfulfilled desire for nurture, love, acceptance, and belonging, and they vow that what happened to them in childhood will never happen again. Their solution is to build psychological walls and to develop behaviors that keep everyone at a "safe" mental and emotional distance. Their logic assumes that self-protection by isolation will be less painful than continued rejection and abandonment. Tragically, while alone in their self-imposed seclusion, they are often accompanied by their own harsh inner critic who is far more pervasive and dangerous than the people they are trying to avoid. To make matters worse, their lack of close and meaningful relationships prevents others from speaking God's truth and wisdom into their life. As such, despite their best efforts at self-protection, life becomes even more difficult, lonely, and silently painful.

The point of walking you through the childhood training program is to show you that many difficulties in life begin early and are linked directly to people. It is often the actions of our parents, caregivers, childhood peers, and others, and what they say about us, uplifting or condemning, that shape our early thoughts about life and the value we place on ourselves. It is critical to understand that, any lack of value placed on us by them, or their words of condemnation, were injected into our minds without our understanding or permission, and it is from these building materials that we initially construct our self-esteem and agendas for relating to others. A poor self-esteem and a life of difficult relationships often makes perfect sense in light of the building materials that were available in childhood, and a child's limited ability when it comes to understanding and constructing such complex structures. The good news is that God is most excellent at remodeling and He provides for our healing and renewal.

Questions

1) What agendas did you establish as you emerged from childhood? Are those agendas helpful in your relationships?

2) What are the agendas of others with whom you are now in relationship?

God's Provision

When difficulties begin in a childhood filled with loneliness, ridicule, or abandonment, where is God's provision of a family? If a difficult childhood consists of feeling worthless and unloved, where is God's provision of value? If flawed parents, caregivers, or peers built hostile structures of condemnation on the sacred ground of a child's mind, where is God's provision for renewal?

God's provision addresses our needs at all levels. First, He offers salvation through His Son Jesus, who will never leave us or forsake us. Second, He unites us with a family of believers who are His body. Third, He provides healing and renewal through the power of the Holy Spirit. Fourth, He provides wise counsel, guidance, and comfort through other believers. And fifth, He confronts any lies we were taught in childhood with His Son Jesus, who offers to replace the world's yoke of deceiving lies with His yoke of renewing truth. And if we accept Jesus as our yoke, we can learn from Him and find rest for our soul.

Jesus teaches us that we are not stupid because we know Him. He teaches us that in our weakness He is made strong, and He is our strength. He also teaches us that we are loved and worthy of being born because we are precious in His sight, and that He has a purpose for us. He teaches us that we are of great value, so much so that He purchased us with His blood when He suffered, died on the cross, and rose again. He also provides us with the love, acceptance, and belonging that we desire throughout our life, not only during childhood. When others fail us, He does not.

For those who did not have positive role models in childhood, or do not have a supportive family, God provides a new family of believers who can serve that purpose. From His family we can ask fellow believers with experience to accompany us on our path as we give them permission to speak words of wisdom, encouragement, and if needed, accountability into our life. While hearing, believing, and acting on these words can feel uncomfortable at first, think about how amazing it is when someone who has had a difficult childhood takes a stand and stops the legacy of pain and sadness that they received from being passed on unchallenged to their loved ones.

If your childhood was difficult, work hard to recover what was lost so you can build a new legacy of hope, wisdom, and love for your children and others whom you will mentor. Make this happen with God's help through the power of the Holy Spirit. You are the vegetable garden created from a vacant lot, and your future harvest depends on you receiving Jesus as your yoke and yielding to him as your gardener. Let Him heal and work through you.

When Jesus invites you to come and take His yoke, He is offering you the provision of being united with Him. Once you accept Him as your Savior, all of God's provision is yours through Him. He begins with a renewing of your mind by tearing down any lies that were built into you by uninvited squatters. Once again, what was originally built without your understanding or permission is rebuilt with Jesus' truth and your intent. The outcome is that you continue to work out your salvation with God "… who works in you to will and to act in order to fulfill his good purpose" (Philippians 2:13). The beginning of that work is to exchange the bondage of childhood agendas for the freedom of Jesus, so you can learn from Him and enter into His rest as you discover what God's planned purposes are for you. God's first purpose for all of us is to become His temple.

Temple of the Holy Spirit

The Apostle Paul wrote to the Corinthians about the relationship between their body and Jesus.

> 15 Do you not know that your bodies are members of Christ himself? Shall I then take the members of Christ and unite them with a prostitute? Never! 16 Do you not know that he who unites himself with a prostitute is one with her in body? For it is said, "The two will become one flesh." 17 But whoever is united with the Lord is one with him in spirit.

> 18 Flee from sexual immorality. All other sins a person commits are outside the body, but whoever sins sexually, sins against their own body. 19 Do you not know that your bodies are temples of the Holy Spirit,

who is in you, whom you have received from God?
You are not your own; [20] you were bought at a price.
Therefore honor God with your bodies. (1 Corinthians
6:15-20)

The oneness of a Christian with Jesus is made clear in verse 15
with the question, "Do you not know that your bodies are
members of Christ himself?" And in verse 17 he continues, "But
whoever is united with the Lord is one with him in spirit." These
are strong statements about our body being a member of Jesus,
and our spirit being united with Him. Paul emphasizes the
importance and purpose of our body even more in verses 19 and
20 where he refers to our bodies as "temples of the Holy Spirit,"
and calls us to "honor God with your bodies."

I don't know about you, but when I look into a full-length
mirror, the phrase "temple of the Holy Spirit" is not the first
thought that comes to mind. My problem is that I usually see with
earthly eyes, not God's eyes. I see the physical creation of Mary
Lucile Martin and William (Bill) Dennis Mills. I also see my inner
self that is far from temple material. I hear not only my thoughts
of love, peace, and joy, but also those of jealousy, pride, and envy.
I often see the value or lack of value that others place *on* me, rather
than the value of the Holy Spirit that God placed *in* me. In
response to Paul's statement, when I ask myself, "What can I do to
honor God with my body?" I hear a harsh clanging thought that
says, "Nothing," which is thankfully true when I remember what
Jesus said in John 15:5, "…apart from Me you can do nothing."

To recap, we are trained by others at an early age without our
understanding or permission. Based on these experiences we
emerge from childhood with agendas for thriving and/or
surviving. God provides us with His Son, a family of believers,
and the Holy Spirit to help us grow into whom He intends us to
be. Once we accept Jesus as the sacrifice for our sins, we become a
living temple of the Holy Spirit. In the next chapter I will explore
the physical characteristics of your temple, which is the ox.

Questions

1) What legacy of healing, wisdom, and hope do you want to build and pass on to your loved ones?

2) Are you a temple of the Holy Spirit? If not, now would be a great time for a grand opening. One way is to believe and say,

> "Jesus, I confess my sins to you, and accept you as my Savior and Lord. Please fill me with your Holy Spirit."

If that is your commitment, find a healthy church where you can join a family of believers who can help equip you for your new journey and accompany you on your path.

CHAPTER 4

Your Ox

Your Original Relationship With Your Ox

Our physical body is represented by the ox, and the driver is our thoughts, will, and emotions. Before becoming a Christian, the driver and the ox enjoy an unchallenged oneness serving each other and honoring only themselves. When all is going well, the driver serves the ox by feeding it what it wants, keeping it as warm or cool as it wants, and making it feel as good as possible whenever possible. The ox serves the driver by pulling the cart to wherever the driver wants and doing whatever is necessary to satisfy the driver's mental, emotional, and physical desires.

For some drivers, the mutually accepting and nurturing oneness of their mind and body relationship has long since eroded. These drivers despise their ox through no fault of its own. It just happens to be too little of one thing or too much of another. If a man's ox is 5 feet 10 inches tall, it cannot fulfill his desire to be a center in the National Basketball Association. And those men and women with too much ox are not going to win any Olympic diving contests as long as judges keep deducting points for a splash. There also is the lifelong beauty contest in which a woman strives to be the most attractive and desired of anyone in the room.

For people who depend on the approval of others, or live with the echoes of destructive condemnations from parents, caregivers, or childhood peers, satisfaction with their ox is nearly impossible. Even if they can drop a basketball straight down through a hoop from a standing position, or if they can enter the water like a beam of light, or if they can walk through a crowd with everyone following their movement the way heads of sunflowers follow the sun, self-acceptance is rarely the result. No feat or physical appearance is ever good enough. The man will be dismayed that the ball was not perfectly centered in the hoop as it went through. The divers will be frustrated when the very thought of a splash causes them to lose points in their mind, and the woman will search her entire body until she finds a single skin pore that is not the same diameter as the others.

The ox and driver relationship gets even worse when the driver uses non-food drugs to silence his or her thoughts of self-condemnation, or to deaden emotional pain that often has been there since childhood. A tipping point is reached when their body becomes addicted and demands to be fed the drug, and if denied, the driver experiences the unrestrained rage of the beast. The body stops fulfilling the desires of the driver, and it demands that the driver satisfy its continual cravings. The driver ends up pulling the cart with the ox sitting on the seat, and the whip of the ox on the back of the driver is far harsher than the driver's ever was. The ox demands everything right up to and including death because it stopped caring about living long ago.

Questions

1) How is your relationship with your ox?

2) Are your choices helping or hurting the beast? If hurting, what different choices can you make?

God Offers a Better Relationship

God offers a better relationship between an ox and its driver. After becoming a Christian, the ox and driver are asked to remake a new oneness in order to serve and honor God. They are asked to stop their devoted dance of self-serving mutual fulfillment. The driver is asked to make choices that will result in storing treasures in heaven, rather than pursuing only pleasures on earth. In addition, the driver is asked to bring the flesh of the ox into submission, rather than serve its never ending desires. The driver and ox are asked to form a new oneness in Jesus as a member of His body with the driver not only taking the yoke of Jesus, but His mind as well. As the Apostle Paul writes in Romans,

> Therefore, I urge you, brothers and sisters, in view of God's mercy, to offer your bodies as a living sacrifice, holy and pleasing to God—this is your true and proper worship. [2] Do not conform to the pattern of this world, but be transformed by the renewing of your mind. Then you will be able to test and approve what God's will is—his good, pleasing and perfect will. (Romans 12:1-2)

Paul is asking us as drivers to stop being conformed to the ways and values of the world, and to worship God as a living sacrifice. When we do, our mind will be renewed and able to test and approve what God's will is.

Questions

1) What does "offer your bodies as a living sacrifice" mean to you?

2) How often do you offer your body as a living sacrifice to God? Do you offer it to others? If so, what are you hoping to receive from them in return?

3) If you could renew your mind, what thoughts and attitudes would you change?

4) When you present yourself as a living sacrifice, don't forget to bring the thoughts and attitudes you listed in question three.

Fearfully and Wonderfully Made?

Not every ox is born *healthy as an ox*.In the Book of Psalms (139:13-18) it is written,

> ¹³ For you created my inmost being;
>   you knit me together in my mother's womb.
> ¹⁴ I praise you because
> I am fearfully and wonderfully made;
>   your works are wonderful,
>   I know that full well.
> ¹⁵ My frame was not hidden from you
>   when I was made in the secret place,
>   when I was woven together in the depths of the earth.
> ¹⁶ Your eyes saw my unformed body;
>   all the days ordained for me were written in your book
>   before one of them came to be.
> ¹⁷ How precious to me are your thoughts, God!
>   How vast is the sum of them!
> ¹⁸ Were I to count them,
>   they would outnumber the grains of sand —
>   when I awake, I am still with you. (Psalm 139:13-18)

It is easy to be inspired by this passage if you are pleased with God's expression of His workmanship in you. However, if you are born with a birth defect or a genetic makeup that you do not like and perhaps despise, this passage can be difficult to accept.

The phrases "knit me together" and "Your eyes saw my unformed body" can be extremely difficult for some parents. "Which way was God looking when He did not give my baby eyes that could see?" Or for that matter, "What was God thinking when He forgot to give my baby a healthy brain?" And if you were born with fetal alcohol syndrome, or a drug addiction because your first dealer was your mother while you were in her womb, you might ask, "Where was God when I was defenseless and needed protection?" My honest answer is, "I don't know."

What I do know from Scripture is that the world we live in is not functioning the way God originally intended. Even though He foreknew and provides for the consequences of the fall, He did not cause it. I still believe God when He says, "As the heavens are higher than the earth, so are my ways higher than your ways and my thoughts than your thoughts" (Isaiah 55:9). It seems clear to me that God often intervenes in our lives according to His *causal* will, which is what he causes to happen. He also can appear to not intervene according to His *permissive* will in that He allows painful and difficult events to happen. Otherwise, I cannot imagine Him causing a pregnant woman to have another beer, even though He allows the free will He gave her to choose to do so.

What I can imagine is that we live in a world where God's love, grace, and judgment provide for the difficult circumstances we face in a way that makes eternal sense of our disappointments, pain, and even our devastation. I am not exactly sure what the reward structure will be when Jesus comes back to stop this madness, but I do recall it being recorded in the Gospels of Matthew, Mark, and Luke that He said something about *the first being last and the last being first*. There will be many in line whose pain and suffering places them far ahead of me.

In the next chapter we will consider why and how you should care for your ox.

Questions

1) How pleased are you with God's workmanship in you? What might He see that you are overlooking?

2) How difficult is it to fully embrace God and His provision for your sin if you do not fully embrace His provision of your body?

CHAPTER 5
'One Mores' and 'Not Yets'

When your ox dies, your cart stops, and your temple is closed.

The Apostle Paul writes "Let each of you look not only to his own interests, but also to the interests of others" (Philippians 2:4, ESV). Notice the "not only," which is not included in the New International Version. I prefer this translation of the verse because if you do not also look out for your own interests, how else will you keep your temple of the Holy Spirit open for God's purposes. Besides, there is that *Love your neighbor as yourself* theme that weaves its way throughout Scripture. Many neighbors would not put up with being loved and treated in the same way some Christians love and treat themselves. And finally, what use is it to be "as shrewd as snakes" and "as innocent as doves" if it is not to look out for your own interests in addition to those of others.

Questions

1) Does the thought of looking out for *your own interests* feel foreign to you? If so, why?

2) Does the thought of looking out for *the interests of others* feel foreign to you? If so, why?

3) Would your neighbors be satisfied receiving from you the same love you have for yourself? If not, did others teach you not to love yourself? If so, which of God's truths were their lessons based on?

Our 'One Mores' and 'Not Yets'

Save for a few notable exceptions in the Bible and when our Lord returns, everyone on this earth is headed for physical death, and when that happens for a Christian, his or her temple of the Holy Spirit will be closed. And when that happens for you, my question is, "How many *one mores* and *not yets* will be left waiting at your temple door?"

A *one more* is what you will want one more of just before you die. One more hug from your spouse or child. One more chance to tell a parent or friend how much you love and appreciate them. One more chance to sit with family members after a meal and share stories that get embellished over the years. One more chance to make a difference in someone's life. One more chance to feed a hungry child or comfort someone who has a broken heart.

Think about what your *one mores* will be, and give as many of them as you can before your temple is closed. I use the word "give" rather than "get" because the *one mores* I have mentioned are not only a gift from God to you, they are also a gift to the people who receive them from you. One more hug from you. One more kind word from you. One more meal or prayer.

A *not yet* is something in the future that you are not yet able to do such as start a career, get married, become a parent, or watch your daughter or son graduate. Perhaps these *not yets* are for you to enjoy with your granddaughter or grandson. Maybe your *not yet* is a ministry you want to start, or one in which you want to serve. While many *not yets* are stolen from us by circumstances, illness, or age, we should strive to not let any die unnecessarily from a lifetime of neglect, fears, and excuses.

Questions

1) What will your *one mores* be?

2) What could you do today to give one more of your *one mores*?

3) What are your *not yets* that are worth taking care of yourself and living for?

Freddie

My life changing lesson in *one mores* came while I was a practicing veterinarian and was examining a growth on the side of a dog's chest. The lesson came as a single question from the dog's owner. Before I reveal the question, let's step out of the examination room so I can give you some background.

I bought my first veterinary hospital from Dr. Frederick E. Leach in Virginia Beach, Virginia. He began his career as a small boy who, wearing a floor-length smock, escorted clients and their pets to the examination rooms for his father. When he started his own veterinary clinic he listed his father's name above his own because as he told me, "I owe everything I am to him."

Freddie and I began a lifelong friendship that lasted a little over a year because he died of leukemia at the age of thirty-five. His mother was constantly at his side, and did everything in her power to save him. She would have gladly traded her life for his.

The last time Freddie and I spoke was over the phone while he was in isolation and undergoing therapy. I could hear how weary he was and I told him I was sorry that he had to go through so much pain from the treatments. His immediate response was, "The pain is nothing compared to the thought of leaving my son." The call was short and I told him that I loved him, appreciated all that he had done for me and my family, and that I would be praying for him. The last thing he said to me was, "I'll see you later."

Let's step back into the examination room for my client's question.

I asked if her dog had previously developed any similar growths to which she replied, "Yes, he had one taken off by Dr ... what's his name? You know, Dr ... Dr ... Ohhh ... what's his name?" As she was searching for his name I leaned back against the counter and the sound of her voice faded as my thoughts grew louder.

"What's his name?" I repeated to myself. "What's his name! You were a 10% discount client who he came in after-hours for, and you cannot even remember his name!! What's his name!!!" I leaned forward slightly, and asked softly, "Freddie?" She replied, "Yeah, yeah, yeah, Dr. Leach."

Now I don't mean to put my client in a bad light because I forget names with the best of them – sometimes momentarily even the names of my daughters. That said, on the drive home that night I could not help but think that today I was Doctor Mills, and someday I would be Doctor What's his name? Was I going to be Daddy What's his name? or Husband What's his name? or even worse, stand in front of the mirror someday and see, What's his name?

It was not until several years later I understood that my real question was, "Are the professional *one mores* I am doing today worth trading another day of my life, and possibly turning my *not yets* into *not evers*?" I have to confess that even now, some days are better trades than others. Some of my best trades, however, were the years of lunches after Freddie's passing I had with his father and mother, and the times visiting them after we moved away from Virginia Beach. When we are together we laugh and often cry as we remember Freddie and think about the *one mores* we never had. My point is that you should seize all of the *one mores* with your loved ones that you can, while you can, because there will come a day when your temple or their temple will be closed.

When I stand before Jesus and He examines my life, I think He will be very interested in the impact of my life on the lives of those around me. I think He will be looking at those lives closely to see if He can find any *one mores* of ours in them. I use the word "ours" because they are His *one mores* through me as well.

When it comes to the *one mores* He will be looking for, there are many you and I could think of. Think of an adult in the future who will read better because you are teaching him today while he is a child. Think of a single mother who now has groceries and someone to talk with because you choose to stand with her rather than abandon her as someone else did. Think of a young athlete who you speak ability into and practice with. Think of the people who experience tragedies that you cannot change other than to make sure they are not alone when they go through them. Think of all the things Jesus would do if He could only be there in person. Then think of the fact that He is – in you.

I've used the word "think" a lot because you are responsible for the intentional choices you make in how you invest your life. This is important because your choices matter not only to you, but also to Jesus and those around you.

With all of your *one mores* and *not yets* at stake, along with Jesus' *one mores* and *not yets* through you, it makes sense to take care of your body. I have no doubt that if you could see all that God has prepared for you to do in the future, you would do everything in your power to keep your temple of the Holy Spirit open for as long as possible. Ultimately, however, your temple may be closed much earlier than you and your friends and family want, as it was for Freddie. As such, it is wise for you to enjoy each day that you are given without trading it for *one more worry* or allowing it to be consumed by a *fear-filled not yet*.

Worry
Many times we imagine far into the future through the lens of our wounds and disappointments. The *one mores* and *not yets* in these painful predictions can feel unbearable when the presence of Jesus is not included. The problem is that God's grace is offered in our reality at the moment we need it, and we usually fail to include it when we are thinking/worrying about the future. So, if your mind happens to wonder into the future, don't forget to take Jesus with you.

Allowing your mind to dwell in a dark future is not without consequence to your body. It often cannot tell the difference between thoughts and reality, so it responds to the stress of thoughts as though they actually happened. Mark Twain once said, "I am an old man and have known a great many troubles, but most of them never happened." Thinking about the future with Jesus in it is fine, however, immersing yourself in dark predictions without Him will eventually deplete you of all hope, and rob you of any possibility of experiencing joy. And if these dark predictions take hold in your mind, you may as well place a sign on your temple door that says,

> Out for worry.
> Not sure when or if I will be back.

The Apostle Paul addressed worry and anxiety in his letter to the Philippians.

> [4] Rejoice in the Lord always. I will say it again: Rejoice! [5] Let your gentleness be evident to all. The Lord is near. [6] Do not be anxious about anything, but in every situation, by prayer and petition, with thanksgiving, present your requests to God. [7] And the peace of God, which transcends all understanding, will guard your hearts and your minds in Christ Jesus.
>
> [8] Finally, brothers and sisters, whatever is true, whatever is noble, whatever is right, whatever is pure, whatever is lovely, whatever is admirable—if anything is excellent or praiseworthy—think about such things. [9] Whatever you have learned or received or heard from me, or seen in me—put it into practice. And the God of peace will be with you. (Philippians 4:4-9)

Not a lot more to say other than you might want to read it again.

Questions

1) What *one mores* are you doing that make a difference to others?

2) Have wounds and disappointments caused you to lock the door of your temple in order to keep others out? If so, what could a reopening look and feel like to you? To them?

3) If you open your temple to others, what is the chance you will be wounded and disappointed? The answer is 100%. Do you believe that Jesus is *God-enough* to heal and restore you? After all, He is familiar with being repeatedly wounded and disappointed.

CHAPTER 6

Caring for Your Ox

Proverbs 12:10 says, "The righteous care for the needs of their animals, but the kindest acts of the wicked are cruel." I know this does not refer to your body, but I'm a veterinarian and I just could not help including it. Of course, if it is true that caring for your animals is righteous, then caring for people must be right up there as well. And while you are at it, don't forget to care for yourself.

Stigma of Age

If it has not already happened, someday you will notice that the only commercials with actors your age are about arthritis, reverse mortgages, and absorbent undergarments. That is when you may ask yourself, "What have I been doing all of these years? Where did the time go? For what did I trade my life?"

It often is the case that people who are young think they will always be young, and when they are old they think they will always be old. This is not true for believers whose hope is to receive a new body and to live with Jesus eternally. But until then, getting older is what it is.

Getting older means that every day comes and goes with no replays or do-overs. If you need wisdom for one day and do not have it, you at least can learn it and have it for the next. If you fail to learn it, you will be given painful opportunity after painful opportunity to do so, unless perhaps the lesson is about a poisonous snake that Jesus said to be shrewder than.

Do everything you can to redeem each day, both for what it is and what it can be. Do not compromise your health with worry, or by being angry and bitter over the time you think you have wasted or that others have stolen from you. If you choose to remain mired in anger and bitterness about past events, you are only committing the same act of time-thievery against yourself that others have, and your body will suffer for it.

So, when it comes to getting older, take care of your ox and do not despise its changes. If you care for it wisely, honor its age, and drive your cart within its ability, your ox will keep your temple of the Holy Spirit open for yourself and others as long as possible. If you don't, it can't.

Questions for Those With an Older Ox

1) Are you despising your aging ox? If so, how is that getting you and Jesus any more of your *one mores,* or making a difference in the lives of others?

2) What can you do to be kinder to your aging body?

Healing

Recall in Matthew 10 that Jesus gave the apostles authority to "heal every disease and sickness." I firmly believe that Jesus heals people today through the power of the Holy Spirit. What gets confusing is that sometimes He does not. What then gets irritating is religious leaders who claim that a person "did not have enough faith to be healed." I guess according to them you can have enough faith to send money, but not enough to be healed. So if someone lays hands on you and you do not get healed, he or she might claim, "You did not have enough faith!" This blaming-the-victim mentality is never helpful. It does seem odd, however, that when healing does not occur, these "healers" rarely ask themselves why they did not have enough faith to heal you. After all, Jesus did not say to His disciples, "heal every disease and sickness of those who have enough faith for you to do so."

Call the Veterinarian for Your Ox

The type of physicians that Christians seek varies considerably. Some Christians care only that their physicians are saved, or perhaps that they attend the same church. Other Christians could not care less about the spirituality or church affiliation of their physicians as long as they are the best qualified based solely on medical ability. For me, the ideal is a physician with strong medical ability, who prays for patients, and is sensitive to the voice and working of the Holy Spirit. Whichever you prefer, remember that caring for your ox is your responsibility, and it is about keeping your temple of the Holy Spirit open for as long as possible. After all, there are a lot of *one mores* and *not yets* at stake.

A Personal Confession: Do Not Try This at Home

I have added this section after the book was all but finished because I do not want others to go through a similar event. If you have lost a loved one to what follows, I am sorry for your pain, and I include this section to hopefully prevent someone else from having to endure a similar grief as your own.

On January 5, 2015, I experienced significant shortness of breath after running up and down a flight of stairs – twice. While I was bent over at the kitchen counter gasping for air, I kept assuring my wife that I was fine. I started to feel weak, and as I finally laid down on the floor I said to her, "I don't think I'm fine." I lost consciousness, convulsed, and turned a pale blue. She immediately called 9-1-1 and attended to my needs with the help of a friend who had just arrived for a coaching appointment. As I was regaining consciousness, I could hear my friend repeatedly saying, "Come back. Stay here. Stay with us." I recall trying to figure out where I had gone.

Seven days earlier, I had developed a persistent pain in my left calf muscle along with mildly labored breathing on exertion. I ignored these symptoms due to a personally imposed deadline for finishing this book. As it turns out, the pain was caused by a blood clot that had been shedding smaller clots into my lungs during the week prior to my collapse. Finally, a large portion broke off and became a saddle thrombus in my pulmonary artery, which caused me to go into acute respiratory failure. A physician told me later that this type of clot was one of the "widow makers."

I spent four days in ICU, and when I left, the Holy Spirit said, "Life first, work second." Since then, celebrating the Lord's supper with my wife is sweeter and slower, and my quiet time with Jesus is quieter on my part. My goals are more like a stretchy fabric, than the coffin that the deadline for this book almost became.

My obvious confession is that I ignored my ox, and my wife who wanted me to go to the doctor sooner. We almost missed out on all of our *one mores* and *not yets* together, and any other books I hope to write. Lest you think this type of clot is an unusual occurrence, it happens often to people who do not exercise their legs on long airline flights, who have recently had orthopedic surgery, or like me, sit behind a desk for hours on end writing books and software.

There are many *widow* and *widower makers* on your path, and you need to be shrewder than all of them. So TAKE CARE OF YOUR OX!!! Now let's return to the regularly scheduled writing.

Stigma of Illness

It is difficult for some Christians to accept chronic conditions such as diabetes or asthma. This was not a problem for Christians of three or more generations ago because these conditions often caused death at an early age. Today, most use insulin or inhalers without complaining, though they would prefer not having to do so. While these conditions are usually not stigmatized by other Christians, sadly, the same is often not true for mental disorders.

Mental Disorders

The brain is just as much a part of the body as the other organs, and may need supplemental or replacement medication to function properly. Some of these medications are only needed temporarily for a particularly difficult time, such as seasonal affective disorder which is due to inadequate exposure to sunlight in the winter, prolonged unemployment, a divorce, or the death of a spouse or child. Other medications are needed continuously, which is no different than using insulin to treat diabetes.

Many people resist taking the medication their brain needs due to fears of dependency, an alteration of their personality, or the potential for social stigma, which they may have previously inflicted on others. I understand that these medications can be misused, but think about what people are asking themselves or others to do by refusing to take them when needed. In the face of problems such as severe anxiety, depression, or intense grief, they are asking their brain to heal itself of its own illness, or to stand alone against overwhelming circumstances. This would be absurd when applied to other parts of the body.

For example, hikers see no problem using hiking boots in rough terrain, and if you had a broken ankle, you would not walk on it without support and still expect it to heal. Certainly, no one would criticize you for using a cane or crutches. It is the same for supportive medication for the brain when combined with effective counseling or psychotherapy. I have heard others condemn the use of these medications by saying they are "just a crutch." My response is, "Yes, and fortunately for you these medications are a 'crutch' that you do not happen to need." Everyone needs what they need when they need it, and no one needs graceless judgment. The bottom line is that a brain needs what it needs to think, and especially for some conditions, when it thinks it does not.

Questions

1) Are you worth taking care of? If not, who taught you that? Could they have been wrong? Could they convince Jesus that they were correct in their opinion of you?

2) What are the benefits of not caring for yourself?

3) Are you taking care of your brain and the rest of your body? If not, what could you do differently today?

Physical Trauma

[Note: Before I continue, I should tell you that I have no direct personal experience with severe physical trauma and the recovery process. I have watched my father, who was an amazing inventor, suffer from a series of debilitating strokes, and I saw the mental anguish in his eyes when he could remember his invention, but could not explain how it worked. I also watched my mother do everything in her power to stop his gradual and inevitable decline. It was as if he had fallen into a deep well with a rope tied around him. Despite the half of his body that could climb, and all of hers that could pull, he only slipped further and further away until the rope finally broke one morning when he died as she was helping him out of bed. So with my lack of personal experience acknowledged, I will continue.]

While you are responsible for taking care of your temple of the Holy Spirit, accidents, assaults, and trauma can happen despite your best efforts. Whether you are a veteran whose body was maimed by a bullet or an improvised explosive device, or a civilian injured by a drunk driver, or a patient who is recovering from radical surgery to remove a cancer, you are left with a changed physical temple. And depending on the changes, many of your *one mores* may become *never again*, and your *not yets* may become *not ever*. This does not mean, however, there are no more works that God has created in advance for you to do. Jesus will always have His *one mores* and *not yets* to do through you regardless of your physical changes. If He can use a few *loaves and fish* that were presented to Him to feed thousands, He can use all that you present to Him to serve others.

What Is Done, Is Done

When I was fifteen years old, I was walking in the woods behind our home when I saw a two headed cow. It had a head on one end and a head on the other. As I walked closer I realized she was trying to give birth to a calf that was too large for her to do so on her own. I ran to get my dad, and he called the farm manager. Within the hour the three of us were herding her from the woods towards the barn. When we came to a large wooden fence post, the farm manager put a lasso around her neck, wrapped the other end around the post several times and asked me to hold it while he tied smaller ropes to both of the calf's protruding front hooves. Then he and my dad pulled gently and steadily on the ropes until the calf emerged and fell to the ground. The farm manager then took the rope I was holding, unwrapped it from the post, and removed it from the cow's neck. That is when I learned one of life's most difficult lessons. The cow turned and approached her motionless calf that had long since died. She sniffed it twice and licked it once. Then she raised her head, looked around, and started walking back into the woods. *What was done, was done.* When I asked the farm manager why he was letting her go back into the woods he said, "She'll be up at the barn tonight with the others."

After the cow lost her calf, it was easier for her to walk back into the woods because she had no concept of the *not evers* to mourn in the way you or I would. Perhaps you have endured the death of a loved one or experienced the miscarriage of a child, or lost a job, home, or a business. Perhaps you are emerging from a broken relationship or divorce. Whatever tragedy has happened to you, there is a time for withdrawing and mourning, and then a time for returning to the other people in your life. Despite your tragedy, there are people who still need you, many of whom you have not yet met. There are people in the world that Jesus can still minister to through you because they will have to walk the same dark path you have and will need you to help them find their way. Recall that we are all in a war and we are "more than conquerors," and God does not intend for any of us to fight our battles alone.

What Is Not, Is Not

One morning a husband and wife brought me their dog that had escaped from their backyard the day before and had been hit by a car. My patient was a cross between a golden retriever and something taller and skinnier. She was bright and alert, and did not have any injuries other that a shattered left front leg. All of the long bones were broken in many places. Her owners could not afford a referral to a veterinary orthopedic surgeon, and her fractures were well beyond my expertise to repair with the equipment I had available. I suggested we amputate her leg.

At first her owners were shocked, and said that as much as they loved her, they would never put her through that because she would not live a full life. I assured them I once saw a farm dog with an amputated front leg race his owner in a pickup truck down a long lane; the dog did just fine. They accepted the hope that I offered.

The morning after the surgery I arrived early so I could be there when she was let out of her cage. She was in a lower cage that was about eight inches higher than the floor. I opened the door and backed up waiting for her to step out. She stepped out boldly onto her left front leg that was no longer there and fell to the floor landing directly on her incision. Somewhere between her yelp and the gasp of my kennel attendant I pronounced myself to be both stupid and incompetent for not anticipating what had just happened. I used words I will not include here.

After I helped her to stand and balance on her three remaining legs, she looked intently at her incision for about fifteen seconds. Then she looked around the room until she saw the door to the outside. She rocked back slightly on her hind legs, which caused me to react by lunging towards her with open arms. Before I could get in her way, she raised her right front leg and hopped forward like a rabbit. A single hop-step and what a glorious step it was. She looked around and took another and then another. When she finally made it outside, she squatted to urinate, a bit unstable at first, but eventually she figured it out.

She went home the following day, and I can assure you she never stepped out of that kennel on her own again. I was always right there with my *unneeded* open arms. Her trauma and recovery stopped being about her and became laced with my fears and self-condemnation. I was never going to put *myself* through the agony of hearing her in pain again, even though she had already moved past the event and learned on her own how to prevent that from happening agian. She had become *as shrewd as a missing leg*, and I was the only one left with a problem.

When her owners brought her back to have the sutures removed, she was full of life. They said she was "as rambunctious as ever." Her list of *one mores* with her owners was almost completely restored. She taught me that *what is not there, is not there*.

Sometimes God's will for us is to accept *what is* or *what is not*, and to move forward with our lives. There is a time for mourning and a time for letting go to continue living. I am reminded of a quote by Arthur Ashe, a World Number 1 ranked African-American professional tennis player. "Start where you are. Use what you have. Do what you can."

Despite any tragedy you have endured, there are people who still need you, many of whom you have not yet met. There are people in the world that Jesus can still minister to through you because they will have to walk the same dark path you have and will need you to help them find their way. This should sound familiar because I've asked you to read it twice. It is a truth of hope that is easy to forget when you are overwhelmed by a loss and are experiencing pain that seems unbearable.

Healing Revisited

When it comes to accepting *what is* or *what is not*, I am not saying that we should not hope and pray for healing and restoration, or that we should not trust God and step out in faith on a leg that *appears* to be missing. With God all things are possible, though sometimes what is not there, is not there – and will never be there. What I am saying is that people can miss having a new life built from what at first seems only to be shattered dreams, but in reality is God's continued knitting and weaving.

If we insist on remaining angry with God about a loss and our pain, and we refuse to move forward, He will let us, knowing that we will miss out on the *one mores* He has for us, and the *one mores* others would have received from us. If He has to, He will find someone else to do what needs to be done. That said, He will always be ready for our "Yes," and He will embrace us with His arms far more quickly and effectively than I did my three-legged patient. His "embrace," however, may not be felt when He wants us to learn to hop-step, and then to run by His grace and to use whatever we have to do whatever He still has planned for us.

If you are experiencing shattered dreams to a depth that light does not travel, reach out to someone and hold on. Keep breathing. If you need medication to ease your pain as you work through your grief – get it! The enemy wants to steal, kill, and destroy your life along with the rest of your *one mores* and *not yets*. While much is written about the price Jesus paid for us, you working through your pain and sadness is the price you pay to eventually help others. You are worth it, and the difference you will make in the lives of others is worth it – especially to them.

Question

1) Which of your difficult experiences can God use to help others through you?

2) Are there any disappointments or "missing legs" that you need to accept in order to move forward with the *one mores* and *not yets* that are waiting for you? If you cannot do so on your own, will you reach out to someone for help?

Perhaps this prayer is a good place to begin.

> "Father God, I do not completely know your mind or your plans for me. I give you my disappointments, loss, and pain to use as you choose. I trust that you will use them to form me into who you want me to be, so I can glorify you and help others who have suffered as I have."

CHAPTER 7

Your Cart

Your cart represents your innate and developed abilities, along with your spiritual gifting. The impact of these on your personal experience can range from a deep satisfaction to continual discontent. The problem with our cart, and our ox for that matter, is that we are not the only ox and cart on the road. We see all manner of oxen and carts, and more often than not, we compare them to our own.

The Most Fearfully and Wonderfully Made

Recall that children and childish adults often get angry when they do not get what they want when they want it. In the case of the cart they received, it may not have the abilities and spiritual gifts they want and admire in others. They may even believe they received a cart of disabilities with no spiritual gifts whatsoever. It is the same problem as not getting the ox they wanted. It isn't enough for their cart to be fearfully and wonderfully made; they want it to be the most fearfully and wonderfully made of all. I first encountered my desire for this in 1966; I was twelve years old.

On the back page of the April issue of Boy's Life was the cart of all carts. It was a Sting Ray Fast Back bicycle. Not the regular Sting Ray – the Fast Back. It had a banana seat, monkey handlebars, and a tall five speed stick shift on the center bar about a foot in front of the seat. It cost $69.95 and I had about $25. It was April, and summer was fast approaching. I tore off the page, folded it carefully, placed it in my back pocket, and devoted myself entirely to the mission of earning $44.95 plus tax.

By June, I had added about $15 to the fund and my prospects for reaching my goal before summer were not good. One evening my mother asked me how much I had saved and I told her the dismal amount. She asked if it would be okay if she and my father made up the difference. To her great credit she made the offer knowing full well that it would immediately quench my recently acquired passion for property maintenance.

The day she was going to pick up my new bicycle after work I got a long distance telephone call from her. She said, "I'm at the bike shop and I forgot to ask you what color you wanted." Relieved that the purchase of all purchases was still on track I asked, "What colors do they have?" She started listing them and when she said "Black" I said, "Yes!" Nothing was cooler than black.

The first ride that evening did not go as planned. I tried to change gears, but nothing happened because I did not know I was supposed to keep pedaling when I moved the gear shift. When I finally figured that out, and the gears did change, there was a terrible grinding sound because as I also had not yet learned, I was not supposed to pedal hard when changing gears. While I was looking down and fiddling with the gear shift to the sound of grinding sprockets, my right pant leg got caught in the chain. This forced my foot off of the pedal, which caused me to swerve and run straight into the curb. That is when I learned that a tall stick shift on the center bar between the seat and the handlebars is a bad idea.

Eventually my new bike and I worked out our relationship with one another. It wasn't long before I was cruising through the neighborhood with the wind blowing through my quarter-inch burr haircut. I was free as a bird – a cool bird.

And then it happened. It was just like any other day of feeling cool on my bike when a kid rode up on "The Rail." It was lower to the ground, the handlebars were at a different angle, and it was way cooler than my Fast Back. The engineers had even fixed the obvious design flaw by using a stick shift that was much shorter.

The Rail was really cool – cooler than I was. It was not black; it was a cooler gold. And the kid riding it was cooler than I was because he had long hair like the motorcycle riders.

When I saw "The Rail" and this cool kid riding it, things were immediately different between me and my bike. It had broken our unwritten contract to make me the coolest kid in the neighborhood. I acted out my disappointment by no longer polishing its fenders, and I didn't care if it was left out in the rain. I stopped bothering to shift gears, choosing instead to leave it in fifth and pedal slowly until it got up to speed. I had lost my feeling of coolest-ness along with all of the *one mores* with my bike for the rest of the summer.

No more coming out of the house in the morning with pride and excitement to see the coolest bike. No more satisfaction of being able to shift gears without grinding or slipping. No more feeling free as a bird. Just the *bondage of disappointment* in knowing I had a Fast Back and not "The Rail." I never told my parents because they had sacrificed to get me what I wanted when I wanted it. Unknown to them, what I was really trying to buy was much more than transportation.

The following spring I heard rumors that the shorter stick shift of "The Rail" made it more difficult to reach, so kids were just leaving it in fifth gear. I also heard that being lower to the ground resulted in it being more difficult to pedal and not quite as fast. The real problem was that any bike would have broken the same contract of coolest-ness by not being and remaining the most fearfully and wonderfully made as soon as a newer one rolled up.

Questions

1) Do you try to get your "coolness" from things or people like I tried with my "Fast back" bike? If so, does it work? If not, why and what is a better alternative?

2) Can blessings be painful? Which of yours have been, and why?

2) Has God ever blessed you with something you did not want? If so, how did you respond initially and afterwards?

Is your cart wonderfully made?

What kind of cart did God buy you? Remember, Jesus paid a price. Are you smart? Is it easy for you to learn? Do you have a cart with empathy inside? Can you listen to someone's pain and speak hope to them? Can you sing or play an instrument? What happens when you encounter people who are smarter and do not have to work as hard to learn as you do. Or what about those who have more empathy than you, or can speak amazing wisdom into someone's life? What about those who can sing or play an instrument better than you?

If you are not "the best" at the abilities and gifts God has provided, please do not give up on His *one mores* that are planned for your life and the lives of others through you. One more word of encouragement, or one more song, or one more chance to speak wisdom into someone's life. Please, for the sake of these *one mores* and many others that people are counting on from you, do not forget what the Apostle Paul wrote to the believers in Rome.

> 3 For by the grace given me I say to every one of you: Do not think of yourself more highly than you ought, but rather think of yourself with sober judgment, in accordance with the faith God has distributed to each of you. 4 For just as each of us has one body with many members, and these members do not all have the same function, 5 so in Christ we, though many, form one body, and each member belongs to all the others. 6 We have different gifts, according to the grace given to each of us. If your gift is prophesying, then prophesy in accordance with your faith; 7 if it is serving, then serve; if it is teaching, then teach; 8 if it is to encourage, then give encouragement; if it is giving, then give generously; if it is to lead, do it diligently; if it is to show mercy, do it cheerfully. (Romans 12:3-8)

Paul's caution to not think of yourself more highly than you ought is only part of the truth. The other part is that you should use "sober judgment" and not think *more lowly* of yourself than you ought. Self-deprecation and self-condemnation are not the same as humility. True humility is fully acknowledging and appreciating the abilities you choose not to be prideful about.

If these words conflict with those of your parents, caregivers, or peers, and you have been thinking less of yourself than what God says about you, it is your decision upon whose words you are going to build the rest of your life. It matters whose words you choose, because a foundation of self-doubt will prevent others from experiencing much of God's love through you by way of the gifts and abilities you have received from Him.

Suppose for example that your ministry is singing or playing an instrument to ease the suffering of patients in hospice care. Are you the best singer in the building? I doubt it. Do you play an instrument better than anyone else? I doubt it. However, for the person who is dying, you are far greater than all of the choirs and orchestras on earth and in heaven combined.

Can you imagine yourself whispering to your dying audience of one, "I need to stop singing because I'm not the best singer?" Or "I should put this instrument away because my notes aren't perfect." What if someone entered the room and said, "You know, I heard you from out in the hall. To be honest, you're not as good as the other singers and musicians." I doubt that you would look down and say, "You're right. I should leave and let this person die alone while you continue to stand in the hallway and do nothing."

Whether you believe it or not, your cart was made wonderfully enough for you and those on your path. You do not have to be the best to be used in the best way. Jesus does not need you to be the best singer for Him to sing through you, and He does not need you to be the best musician for Him to play through you. However, someone who is dying does need the two of you to work together.

It Is Ok to Not Be "The Best" Parent or Caregiver

You do not have to be "the best" parent or caregiver in order to be used by God. If you make a mistake with your child or someone you are caring for, accept it and apologize. Doing so shows him or her how to apologize when he or she makes a mistake or offends someone.

When apologizing to someone, asking for forgiveness can pose a bit of a problem. It can be perceived as you wanting something more from someone you have wronged. If you must bring up forgiveness, one approach is to say, "If you can forgive me I would appreciate it, and if you cannot, I understand." Forgiveness should be a *freewill* *gift* from the person who was offended, not words that he or she is *compelled* to speak to make you feel better. Give the Holy Spirit time to work in him or her, and whatever offense you committed, try really, really hard not to do it again.

The Wheels on Your Cart

The wheels of your cart represent how you experience your path with all of its ups and downs and rocks and potholes that range from barely noticeable to being large enough to swallow your day, month, or even years.

We are born with wheels on our cart that are a lot like square blocks – they do not roll down the path easily. For infants, life is either very good and they let the world go about its business, or very bad and they start crying, and if necessary, scream at the top of their lungs. Sadly for some, when this does not bring others to the rescue, their brilliant little brains eventually adjust by shutting the system down. After all, why waste energy crying if no one comes to help? This understanding is not lost when they become adults and do not think to ask others for help when needed.

If crying gets results, most of us learn less dramatic ways to get our needs met. In addition, we develop a bit of tolerance as we adjust to which of our needs should be met by others, and which we should take care of on our own. Hopefully, we also learn to let others know when they should meet their own needs as well.

As we grow in Christ, we learn how to discern our true needs, and how to gracefully overcome obstacles on our path. We may even develop some shock absorbing springs of acceptance that foster peace in our lives in the midst of severe difficulties. In essence, our square block wheels from infancy and childhood get chipped away and grow into a much rounder shape. This maturing makes our journey through life as smooth as possible, but no smoother. Conversely, if our wheels fail to mature, even a smooth path is an unpleasant ride, and we can be a major source of irritation and difficulty to others who are accompanying us.

Unfortunately, there are people who are dissatisfied with everything on their path, including what is normal. A classic example is someone who goes on a camping trip for the first time with seasoned campers. The fire is too hot, the air is too cold, the ground is too hard, and when he or she finds a dead fly in a boiling pot of beans, everyone hears about it. Thankfully, most people adjust to the "normal" of camping (and life) and the only disturbance from then on is over who gets the next fly. Others, however, persist in temporarily annoying their companions by continually complaining about the heat, the cold, the ground, and the bugs. I say "temporarily" because people who do this are rarely invited to go on another trip.

An example of my own experience as a teenager with learning to adjust to the "normal" of camping was on a week-long canoe and backpack trip in Canada with my father. Half way across a large lake on the first day I asked him what he brought for us to snack on and he said "Raisins." I was considerably irritated because he knew I did not like raisins – or at least I thought he should have known. I told him I did not like raisins. He replied, "Okay," and was strangely silent for about two hours as we continued paddling. I finally broke the silence with another question: "Where are those raisins?" My hunger caused my wheels to become somewhat rounder on that trip, and I learned to really like raisins.

As I mentioned previously, round wheels do not change the path on which we are traveling though they make the ride easier. Square wheels on the other hand make any path difficult. My point is that sometimes our difficult experiences in life are a combination of the path on which we are traveling, and the fact that our wheels have not grown rounded enough. God's purpose for some difficult paths may even be to chip away at our wheels until they are sufficiently rounded for us to embark on the next mission He has prepared for us.

Questions

1) What gifts and abilities has God given you? Listen for any self-critical thoughts while you are considering this question. If you hear any, where do you think they came from? Are they helpful?

2) Who has God used to round your wheels, and how did He use them?

SECTION 3

Your Path

It is easy to picture an oxcart being driven down a dirt road that has two well-worn tracks with grass growing in the center. One can imagine an occasional sign pointing to the driver's destination that includes the number of miles to get there. At each crossing with other paths, there are even more signs with the mileage to many other destinations. Also along the path one can imagine homes and even towns where others have settled, who can offer rest and reliable information about the journey ahead. A believer's path through life is *nothing* like the path I just described.

Your path and life are unique from everyone who has ever been born, or who will ever be born. There is no well-worn dirt road for you to follow, nor are there signs telling you where you will end up or how far it is to the end of your journey. Your surroundings and horizon can range anywhere from a silent featureless prairie or perhaps even a desert, to a noisy bustling city full of flashing signs pointing to enticing distractions. Every step you take is an unmarked intersection with the option of changing direction, unless your circumstances prevent you from doing so. The people you encounter along your path will vary between wanting God's best for you and offering you wise counsel, to seeking their own desires and deceiving you with lies. If there ever was a need for you to be "as shrewd as snakes," it is on your path.

CHAPTER 8

We are All on the Same Path

If all of our paths are unique, what path could we all share? The Apostle Paul speaks to this in Romans.

> 28 And we know that in all things God works for the good of those who love him, who have been called according to his purpose. 29 For those God foreknew he also predestined to be conformed to the image of his Son, that he might be the firstborn among many brothers and sisters. 30 And those he predestined, he also called; those he called, he also justified; those he justified, he also glorified. (Romans 8:28-30)

We all share the same path of being "predestined to be conformed to the image of his Son," which is a gradual and ongoing process that continues throughout our life. This process is only completed when we either die and go to heaven, or Jesus returns for us and brings this world as we know it to an end. Our conformation to the image of Jesus is a destiny to be received, not a destination to be achieved. What is truly amazing is that each of us is being conformed to our own unique image of the same Son.

We are conformed to the image of Jesus when we take Him as our yoke, learn from Him, and allow God to work in and through us. Paul explains that our predestined conformation is our path to justification and glorification. Unfortunately, Christians can remain trapped in seeking their justification and glorification by other means such as self-effort or relying on the opinions and approval of others.

Justification and Glorification

Personal justification ultimately boils down to the questions, "Should I have been born?" and "Am I worthy to exist?" The problem with asking these questions is they beg yet another, "In whose opinion?" If you refuse to accept that God takes great pleasure in your relationship with Him and that your justification is based solely on His Son's sacrifice, you are left with building your justification from your own works and accomplishments, the opinions of others, and your own opinion of yourself – which you originally built during your childhood from the opinions of others.

The problem of basing your self-justification on the opinions of others is at least threefold. First, there are so many "others" in your life to please. Second, few if any of them will be with you on your deathbed while you think about your missing *one mores* and *not evers*. And third, when your life is over and you must give an account of how you lived, none of these "others" will be filling in for Jesus that day and sitting on His judgment seat.

Living your life solely to win the approval of others always leaves you feeling alone, even in a crowd. And worse, if you never discover and mature into who you are meant to be in Christ, you will not even have your authentic self to keep you company. As I mentioned previously, it is one thing to look in the mirror and not see yourself as the temple of the Holy Spirit, and quite another to look into your inner mirror and not know who you are seeing.

Looking to anyone but God for our glorification is equally perilous. We were created for the Holy Spirit to fill and flow through. This flow is an inexhaustible supply that can displace any self-sighted obsession. When we rely on anything but the Holy Spirit to fill us, we are like a giant inflatable Santa Claus, dancing in someone's yard at Christmas until the fan stops blowing. The irony is that even when our self-filling fan is blowing at full speed and we are completely inflated, we usually still feel a sense of emptiness.

If you experience feelings of emptiness from self-justification or self-glorification, it is the perfect time to come to Jesus and take Him as your only yoke so you can learn from him. If you are a Christian and have taken Him as your yoke, remind yourself once again that God is the one who works for your good and justifies you. He is the one who glorifies you for His glory. Once you are established or reestablished in this truth, you can stop doing the *Santa dance* for others and yourself, and you can continue on your path of being conformed to the image of Jesus.

Questions

1) How much energy do you spend pleasing others and seeking their approval? How fulfilling is it?

2) Are there areas in your life that you do the *Santa dance*? How could you live more authentically, and what would that feel like?

3) Have you ever worked hard for an accomplishment that left you feeling empty or less satisfied than you hoped? If so, why did it fail to provide you with what you wanted? Were you seeking your own justification or glorification? What did you really want?

Proverbs 3:5-6

No discussion about our path through life should leave out Proverbs 3:5-6.

> 5 Trust in the Lord with all your heart
>   and lean not on your own understanding;
> 6 in all your ways submit to him,
>   and he will make your paths straight.

A straight path does not rule out straight up steep cliffs or straight down into deep ravines or the darkest of valleys. Psalm 23:4 states, "Even though I walk through the darkest valley, I will fear no evil, for you are with me; your rod and your staff, they comfort me." If dark valleys were not part of a believer's journey, Proverbs 3:6 would have said, "...and he will make your paths straight, level, and smooth," and Psalm 23:4 would not be necessary.

Signs on Your Path

When traveling in the United States, there are a few tourist attractions that advertise on billboards beginning about 100 to 200 miles before you get there. You barely lose sight of one in your rearview mirror before another appears on the horizon. Oh, how I wish the Holy Spirit's voice was as persistently present on our path as those signs. The problem is that if it were, there would be no opportunity for us to develop faith. According to the book of Hebrews, our faith is essential as the author writes, "And without faith it is impossible to please God because anyone who comes to him must believe that he exists and that he rewards those who earnestly seek him" (Hebrews 11:6).

I am not saying that God cannot speak to us through signs in creation or our circumstances, which I think He sometimes does. And I could even convince myself that asking for signs is biblical because God honored Gideon's request for two signs regarding a fleece in Judges Chapter 6. There is a problem, however, when the *seeking of signs* becomes more consuming and comforting than a *sightless faith* that matures as we become more and more conformed to the image of Jesus. An obsession with seeking signs is not one of the works that God prepared in advance for us to do.

Faith and Unbelief

In Chapter 10 of Hebrews, Jesus is presented as the final sacrifice for "sins and lawless acts." Beginning in verse 23, the author calls for us to "hold unswervingly to the hope we profess, for he who promised is faithful" (Hebrews 10:23). The author continues in the first two verses of Chapter 11 with the definition of faith.

> "Now faith is confidence in what we hope for and assurance about what we do not see. ² This is what the ancients were commended for." (Hebrews 11:1-2)

Throughout Chapter 11 the author recounts specific terror-filled events that people in the Old Testament overcame through faith. So, what can we conclude about faith?

First, God is faithful and provides for the consequences of our sins by accepting Jesus as the final sacrifice. Second, there must be some serious difficulties on our path that can cause us to swerve because we are told to hold "unswervingly" to our hope. Third, faith is needed and expected in the midst of terror because faith is what "the ancients" used to overcome many terrifying circumstances. Fourth, faith begins where sight ends. The Apostle Paul makes this distinction between living by faith or by sight when writing to the Corinthian church about his preference for either living on the earth in his body or going to heaven.

> ⁶ Therefore we are always confident and know that as long as we are at home in the body we are away from the Lord. ⁷ For we live by faith, not by sight. ⁸ We are confident, I say, and would prefer to be away from the body and at home with the Lord. (2 Corinthians 5:6-8)

Fifth, even though God performed signs and wonders as recorded in the Old and New Testaments, believers were commended for their faith and their actions that emerged from their faith, not their seeking for, or depending upon signs and wonders.

The role of signs and wonders in the faith of believers was of concern to Jesus as recorded in the Gospel of John when a man asked Him to heal his son. "Unless you people see signs and wonders," Jesus told him, "you will never believe" (John 4:48).

Even so, Jesus understands our difficulty in believing as was recorded in Mark Chapter 9 when a father brought his son to Him for healing. What follows is a portion of their conversation.

[21]Jesus asked the boy's father, "How long has he been like this?"

"From childhood," he answered. [22] "It has often thrown him into fire or water to kill him. But if you can do anything, take pity on us and help us."

[23] "'If you can'?" said Jesus. "Everything is possible for one who believes."

[24] Immediately the boy's father exclaimed, "I do believe; help me overcome my unbelief!"

[25] When Jesus saw that a crowd was running to the scene, he rebuked the impure spirit. "You deaf and mute spirit," he said, "I command you, come out of him and never enter him again."

[26] The spirit shrieked, convulsed him violently and came out. The boy looked so much like a corpse that many said, "He's dead." [27] But Jesus took him by the hand and lifted him to his feet, and he stood up. (Mark 9:21-27)

Jesus did not rebuke or condemn the father for his inner turmoil and mix of belief and unbelief. Neither will He rebuke or condemn us for being honest with Him about our struggle with unbelief and the terror we may experience while traveling on our path. In Mark 9:19, Jesus did, however, express concern about His disciples not being able to heal the boy where it is written,

"You unbelieving generation," Jesus replied, "how long shall I stay with you? How long shall I put up with you? Bring the boy to me." (Mark 9:19)

My point is that your faith and my faith grow as we mature in Christ, and we need to hold on to the truth of,

"Therefore, there is now no condemnation for those who are in Christ Jesus, [2] because through Christ Jesus the law of the Spirit who gives life has set you free from the law of sin and death." (Romans 8:1-2)

Furthermore,

> 8 For it is by grace you have been saved, through faith—and this is not from yourselves, it is the gift of God— 9 not by works, so that no one can boast. 10 For we are God's handiwork, created in Christ Jesus to do good works, which God prepared in advance for us to do. (Ephesians 2:8-10)

It is critical to understand that belief and faith can emerge either from our anxiety-ridden flesh in an effort to drown out the shouting voice of fear in the face of terror, or from our *vine and branch oneness* with Jesus. The first is a *childish* faith, and the second is a *childlike* faith. And guess what? There is no condemnation as our childish faith and our struggle with unbelief matures into a childlike faith that confidently trusts in Him. Jesus only wants you and me to be as honest with Him, and with ourselves, about our unbelief in the same way the sick boy's father was about his. Our honesty begins with presenting ourselves as a living sacrifice, which includes all of our good and not-so-good, along with our belief and unbelief.

> Therefore, I urge you, brothers and sisters, in view of God's mercy, to offer your bodies as a living sacrifice, holy and pleasing to God—this is your true and proper worship. 2 Do not conform to the pattern of this world, but be transformed by the renewing of your mind. Then you will be able to test and approve what God's will is—his good, pleasing and perfect will. (Romans 12:1-2)

When you present yourself as a living sacrifice, the signs or lack of signs on your path will be seen with a transformed and renewed mind that is becoming more closely conformed to the mind of Jesus. You will make better decisions and grow in your ability to "test and approve what God's will is." And when you see *no signs* on your path, you will rely faithfully on the last and sufficient direction that God gave you.

Questions

1) In what ways do you struggle with belief and unbelief? Is it possible that you are a "typical" Christian whose faith is in the process of being conformed to the image of Jesus? Is there anything wrong with being "typical."

2) Is it possible for you to continually present your accomplishments, failures, and yourself as a living sacrifice to God? Will you? Do you think anything you present to God will be a surprise to Him?

CHAPTER 9

God Speaks to You

While it is written in Numbers Chapter 22 that God used a donkey to speak to Balaam, when I am struggling with a decision, my first choice is not to travel from farm to farm looking for advice. There is something similar that is almost as foolish, which is running from friend to friend.

If Jesus wants a vine and branch relationship with you, it makes sense that you should look first to Him, the Bible, and the Holy Spirit for guidance. After that, it is usually a good idea to look for confirmation from other more mature branches of His vine, which are fellow Christians.

In the Gospel of John when Jesus told the disciples He had to leave He said,

> "But the Advocate, the Holy Spirit, whom the Father will send in my name, will teach you all things and will remind you of everything I have said to you. ²⁷ Peace I leave with you; my peace I give you. I do not give to you as the world gives. Do not let your hearts be troubled and do not be afraid." (John 14:26-27)

According to this passage, the Holy Spirit is our advocate and He has a voice with which to teach us all things and remind us of what Jesus has said. And if the Holy Spirit is going to teach and remind, then we can assume that God has given us a means with which to hear Him.

The Apostle Paul also speaks in Romans about the voice of the Holy Spirit.

> 26 In the same way, the Spirit helps us in our weakness. We do not know what we ought to pray for, but the Spirit himself intercedes for us through wordless groans. 27 And he who searches our hearts knows the mind of the Spirit, because the Spirit intercedes for God's people in accordance with the will of God. (Romans 8:26-27)

Is the Holy Spirit Still Active?

Many sincere, fruitful, and loving Christians with effective ministries have a doctrinal deafness when it comes to hearing that the Holy Spirit actively moves in and through us in the same way that He did in the Apostle Paul's generation. For example, I have heard it taught from the following passage that prophesies and tongues have ceased because it was claimed that the "completion" Paul was referring to was the New Testament.

> 8 Love never fails. But where there are prophecies, they will cease; where there are tongues, they will be stilled; where there is knowledge, it will pass away. 9 For we know in part and we prophesy in part, 10 but when completion comes, what is in part disappears. 11 When I was a child, I talked like a child, I thought like a child, I reasoned like a child. When I became a man, I put the ways of childhood behind me. 12 For now we see only a reflection as in a mirror; then we shall see face to face. Now I know in part; then I shall know fully, even as I am fully known. (1 Corinthians 13:8-12)

The reasons for my divergence from those who interpret the assembled New Testament as the "completion" that marked the end of the Holy Spirit's ministry as it was in Paul's generation are at least five-fold. First, when I look at the New Testament I am *seeing a lot*, but I am not seeing "face to face." Second, the New Testament contains a lot of knowledge and wisdom, but not enough for me to "know fully, even as I am fully known." Third, there is no indication that Paul anticipated the final compilation of writings now known as the New Testament, so I doubt that was the "completion" to which he was referring. Fourth, I read where Jesus gives us the Holy Spirit, and I do not find any passage where Jesus takes the Holy Spirit back or replaces Him with something or someone else. And fifth, I do not see where Satan has laid down any of his weapons, so it does not make sense to me that God would have *recalled* any of ours.

A Gift in a Box

A gift in a box, other than a paperweight, cannot be used until it is opened. And just because some charlatans attract attention and steal money with counterfeit imitations of spiritual gifts, that does not mean we should neglect the real ones. After all, the spiritual driving habits of children who either accidentally or intentionally back their *spiritual-gift-cars* over pedestrians should not disqualify the use of spiritual gifts by mature adults. Then again, if a mature adult owned a car and was never told it was in the garage, how could he or she possibly learn how to drive?

When all is said and done, or not done, the active and full participation of the Holy Spirit in our lives is required for us to do what Jesus said His believers would do. He said, "Very truly I tell you, whoever believes in me will do the works I have been doing, and they will do even greater things than these, because I am going to the Father" (John 14:12). Do you ever wonder why we do not see an abundance of these "greater things?"

Flesh and Blood Struggle?

Perhaps the most compelling passage with regard to the Holy Spirit's active participation in our life is the Apostle Paul's famous armor of God passage in Ephesians.

> [10] Finally, be strong in the Lord and in his mighty power. [11] Put on the full armor of God, so that you can take your stand against the devil's schemes. [12] For our struggle is not against flesh and blood, but against the rulers, against the authorities, against the powers of this dark world and against the spiritual forces of evil in the heavenly realms. [13] Therefore put on the full

armor of God, so that when the day of evil comes, you may be able to stand your ground, and after you have done everything, to stand. [14] Stand firm then, with the belt of truth buckled around your waist, with the breastplate of righteousness in place, [15] and with your feet fitted with the readiness that comes from the gospel of peace. [16] In addition to all this, take up the shield of faith, with which you can extinguish all the flaming arrows of the evil one. [17] Take the helmet of salvation and the sword of the Spirit, which is the word of God.

[18] And pray in the Spirit on all occasions with all kinds of prayers and requests. With this in mind, be alert and always keep on praying for all the Lord's people. [19] Pray also for me, that whenever I speak, words may be given me so that I will fearlessly make known the mystery of the gospel, [20] for which I am an ambassador in chains. Pray that I may declare it fearlessly, as I should. (Ephesians 6:10-20)

When Paul talks about "our struggle," he is not referring to something as safe as debating the existence of God with an atheist who hates all Christians and the carts they rode in on. Paul is referring to struggles "against the rulers, against the authorities, against the powers of this dark world and against the spiritual forces of evil in the heavenly realms." These struggles require the full armor of God, not just part of it. This means we need to be "as shrewd as snakes," and not enter into our spiritual battles partially dressed by relying only on the intellectual power of our *flesh and blood* brain.

Paul tells us to "Take the helmet of salvation and the sword of the Spirit, which is the word of God." If by "sword of the Spirit" he meant only the *written* word of God up to and including the completed New Testament, which there is no indication he anticipated, it seems to me he would have clarified his point by adding, "and the sword of the Spirit, which is the Scriptures and all of the letters and teachings I and other leaders have written to the churches, including this one." I am not diminishing at all the importance of knowing and quoting Scripture to defend yourself when you are attacked spiritually because that is what Jesus did when he was tempted in the desert as recorded in Matthew Chapter 4. What I am saying, however, is that *true evil* cannot be successfully debated into submission using only our *flesh and blood* intellect. Standing firm against *true evil* requires that we do so in the authority of Jesus, with the word of God, and the moment-by-moment gifting, leading, and power of the Holy Spirit.

Paul also says in verses 18-20, "[18] And pray in the Spirit on all occasions with all kinds of prayers and requests." And "that whenever I speak, words may be given me so that I will fearlessly make known the mystery of the gospel, [20] for which I am an ambassador in chains." He also taught his followers in Rome about at least one other kind of prayer in which the "Spirit himself intercedes for us through wordless groans" (Romans 8:26). And for the "words" to be given to him, I doubt Paul expected them to come from his own intellect. Rather, words would be given to him in the same way Jesus promised His disciples in Matthew 10 when He said,

> "[19] But when they arrest you, do not worry about what to say or how to say it. At that time you will be given what to say, [20] for it will not be you speaking, but the Spirit of your Father speaking through you. (Matthew 10:19-20)

For those believers who choose not to embrace the ongoing voice, guidance, ministry, and power of the Holy Spirit, and choose to fight against the rulers, authorities, powers of this dark world, and spiritual forces of evil using only the power of their intellect – good luck when it comes to a truly spiritual battle. Even so, it is fortunate for them, and the body of Christ, that God continues to give spiritual gifts to believers who *do not believe* that He continues to give spiritual gifts. That acknowledged, the use of those gifts will be greatly diminished when there is a lack of teaching, understanding, and training in their use.

Is it the Holy Spirit's Voice or is it Mine?

What we hear as guidance from the Holy Spirit can range from a clear directive to a barely audible thought in our mind that may even feel like a subtle intuitive knowing. The most important test, however, is that if the voice you hear is the Holy Spirit, it will never contradict Scripture.

At least three things are important to remember when it comes to hearing the Holy Spirit. First, we must always be on guard that we do not listen only for what we want to hear. Second, confirmation of the Holy Spirit's voice often occurs when we hear the same message from several sources that may include our friends. Third, our spiritual immaturity will not silence the Holy Spirit. Even if we ignore Him, He often repeats the same message out of His love for us and His understanding that we are children. Unfortunately, the message may become no longer relevant if it is an ignored warning about a snake. Even then, and especially then, the Holy Spirit will not abandon us because God foreknew everything we would ever say and do when He first received us.

Silent Presence

For many of us, the most difficult time in life is when we seek guidance, and the Holy Spirit speaks silence. We often forget He is always with us, even when He is silently with us. He is quite comfortable communicating with us on a need-to-know basis. So, when He is silent, we can be certain that we are on a need-to-have-faith basis.

Unfortunately, during the Holy Spirit's silence, we often make the mistake I mentioned earlier which is to anxiously go from friend to friend in an effort to force God's voice from them. Despite this temptation, I suspect that in Deuteronomy 5:7 when God said, "You shall have no other gods before me," He also meant our friends.

A potential danger when asking friends for advice is if their discomfort in seeing us in distress and their desire to help causes them to not first seek the guidance of the Holy Spirit. As a result, they may immediately begin giving us their personal opinion from their *flesh and blood intellect*. Wise friends will pray and wait to hear from the Holy Spirit. Hopefully, if they receive wisdom, they will have the love and boldness to share it, and if they do not, will have the same love and boldness to confirm His silence to them as well.

In closing, it bears repeating that any guidance you think you receive from the Holy Spirit or others must be consistent with Scripture and will usually be confirmed by more than one source.

Questions

1) Can you recall a time when you were absolutely certain that the Holy Spirit spoke to you? How did you know it was His voice, and what did He say? Remembering that time or those times can be a precious handhold when you are assailed by the storms of our enemy.

2) Can you recall a time when the Holy Spirit was *silently with you* for a period of time and finally spoke? Remembering that time or those times when He was *silently faithful* can also be a precious handhold when you are assailed by the storms of our enemy.

CHAPTER 10

Our Mission

Our mission as Christians is not first about what, when, where, or how, but rather is about who: Whose mission? Whose purpose? Whose power? Whose glory?

Who Gets to Be God?

I once read about a sign a veterinarian had posted in His waiting room that said,

> The successful outcome of your pet's healthcare
> may well depend upon
> which one of us gets to be the veterinarian.

I can only imagine his previous debates with clients that caused him to think that the sign was a good idea. After all, the clients he thought should read it obviously believed its message. But what about us? Do we need a sign in God's waiting room that says,

> The successful outcome of your life
> may well depend upon
> which one of us gets to be God.

In Exodus 3:14 when God said to Moses, "I am who I am," He could also have added, "and you are not who I am."

You and I can be amazingly creative. We can think of an idea, plan the steps to make it happen, execute those steps, and have personal satisfaction in the outcome. This ability and our satisfaction with the outcome makes perfect sense because you and I were created in the image of God who creates and takes pleasure in His creation. The important distinction is that we do not use our creativity to perform works *for God, apart from God.* Rather, He works His creativity in and through ours, that He gave us, as we yield it to Him to serve others. For us to be able to do this, we must yield to Jesus as our yoke, and not to an inner yoke of performance.

Who Gets to Make Mistakes?

As we identify and work through the various missions that God has prepared for us, we are often presented with the same question from Chapter 4 about the driver, "Is it me or is it God?"

A dear friend of mine worked the night shift in a doughnut shop in New York City with the goal of sharing the Gospel message with others. After two years, to her knowledge, she had not had a single meaningful conversation with a patron about Jesus. One night she was praying in anguish to the Lord about failing to reach anyone when she heard the Holy Spirit say to her, "You went, I did not send you." She gave her two week notice the next day.

Did she love God? Yes.

Did she act in faith? Yes.

Was she wrong about God's mission? She was told so.

My point is that we are His children, and children make mistakes. I am sure that my friend was used in many other ways during her time at the doughnut shop, though the Holy Spirit made it clear when it was time for her to leave. Recall the Apostle Paul's writing in Romans,

Therefore, there is now no condemnation for those who are in Christ Jesus, 2 because through Christ Jesus the law of the Spirit who gives life has set you free from the law of sin and death. [3] For what the law was powerless to do because it was weakened by the flesh, God did by sending his own Son in the likeness of sinful flesh to be a sin offering. (Romans 8:1-3)

If Jesus can set us free from "the law of sin and death," He can certainly set us free from thinking we have to be *perfectly performing children* in order to earn God's approval.

This idea of not having to be *perfect* to win someone's approval may be inconsistent with your childhood training. Thankfully though, just as God was not created in our image, He was also not created in the image of our parents or caregivers. That is why the journey to discover who God meant for you to be is accompanied by a similar journey for you to discover who God really is to you. A good place to start for those who are dealing with childhood wounds is to understand that God's thoughts are higher than their parents' and caregivers' thoughts. With God, you can make both sincere and insincere mistakes, and still be loved and accepted – even when, and especially when, He disciplines you. And if you still have to face the consequences for your actions, He will never leave you or forsake you.

Questions

1) How have your parents or caregivers influenced your image of God?

2) What would your ideal God do and how would He be when you make mistakes? Is that different from how you view God now? Is that different from how you treat yourself when you make a mistake? If so, who gives you the authority to be harsher than God?

Performance or Relationship

Jesus takes relationships, false prophets, and false disciples personally. He speaks about this in Chapter 7 of Matthew.

> [15] "Watch out for false prophets. They come to you in sheep's clothing, but inwardly they are ferocious wolves. [16] By their fruit you will recognize them. Do people pick grapes from thornbushes, or figs from thistles? [17] Likewise, every good tree bears good fruit, but a bad tree bears bad fruit. [18] A good tree cannot bear bad fruit, and a bad tree cannot bear good fruit. [19] Every tree that does not bear good fruit is cut down and thrown into the fire. [20] Thus, by their fruit you will recognize them.
>
> [21] "Not everyone who says to me, 'Lord, Lord,' will enter the kingdom of heaven, but only the one who does the will of my Father who is in heaven. [22] Many will say to me on that day, 'Lord, Lord, did we not prophesy in your name and in your name drive out demons and in your name perform many miracles?' [23] Then I will tell them plainly, 'I never knew you. Away from me, you evildoers!'" (Matthew 7:15-23)

Jesus states that "every good tree bears good fruit," which is followed by what some would consider to be excellent fruit. Activities like prophesying in His name, driving out demons, and performing miracles sound a lot like what He told His disciples to do in Matthew 10. If these activities are genuine by those He will call "evildoers," what's the problem? He never knew them? Really? With all of the prophecies that need to be spoken, demons that need to be driven out, and all of the miracles that need to be performed, Jesus is going to get hung up with a minor technicality like having a relationship with Him? Yep, that's pretty much it. And that should not come as a shock because He warned His disciples in the vine and branch passage of the Gospel of John that apart from Him they could do nothing, which is true of us as well. Otherwise, fulfilling our mission apart from Him fulfills our own justification and leads to our own glorification.

So how do we prevent spending two years in a doughnut shop where God did not send us, or end up prophesying, driving out demons, and performing miracles, and then spending eternity somewhere we really do not want to be? The answer is not "Do you know *about* Jesus?" or "Does Jesus know *about* you?" but rather, "Does Jesus *know* you?"

Exalting God

Part of knowing God is that we are expected to set aside time to be with Him as the psalmist writes,

> "Be still, and know that I am God;
> I will be exalted among the nations,
> I will be exalted in the earth." (Psalm 46:10)

It is nice to know that God will be exalted among the nations and in the earth, but what matters most is that He is exalted in our heart. This begins with nothing more than *being still*, which is *not doing*. Then comes *knowing*, which is still *not doing*. With that as a foundation, we are ready to enter our oneness and separateness relationship ministry with God as described in Philippians.

> 12 Therefore, my dear friends, as you have always obeyed — not only in my presence, but now much more in my absence — continue to work out your salvation with fear and trembling, 13 for it is God who works in you to will and to act in order to fulfill his good purpose. (Philippians 2:12-13)

God is exalted when He fulfills His purpose in us. This all sounds complicated, something only a trusting imperfect child who makes mistakes could do. Jesus agrees.

> 15 People were also bringing babies to Jesus for him to place his hands on them. When the disciples saw this, they rebuked them. 16 But Jesus called the children to him and said, "Let the little children come to me, and do not hinder them, for the kingdom of God belongs to such as these. 17 Truly I tell you, anyone who will not receive the kingdom of God like a little child will never enter it." (Luke 18:15-17)

My point is, God works through His children who should plan, but not put their faith in plans. He works through His children who should pray, but not put their trust in desired outcomes. He works through His children who present themselves as living sacrifices, not dead priests. And for His children who do not have a mature faith and trust, He works through them as well. What matters is that He *knows* His children and that you *know* Him.

Being Conformed or Remaining Deformed

I remember early in my Christian walk when pastor William (Bill) L. Lane asked me if I wanted God's will for my life. I thought for a moment and said with all sincerity, "I want to want to." He responded with confidence, "God will take that." At the time I had no idea that Jesus receives us as imperfect as we are and breaks us in His hands in the same way He broke loaves and fish. He breaks us in His hands to feed and minister to others. He breaks us in His hands to become His hands in our world. And when He is done breaking, what remains of us is a piece that has been uniquely conformed to His image. If Jesus is doing this, what is there for us to do? The Apostle Paul tells us in Romans, and it should not be new to you by now.

> Therefore, I urge you, brothers and sisters, in view of God's mercy, to offer your bodies as a living sacrifice, holy and pleasing to God—this is your true and proper worship. [2] Do not conform to the pattern of this world, but be transformed by the renewing of your mind. Then you will be able to test and approve what God's will is—his good, pleasing and perfect will. (Romans 12:1-2)

When Paul says, "Do not conform to the pattern of this world" he could also have said, "Do not *remain deformed* to the pattern of this world."

Recall that the first hands we encounter in our life are those of our parents and caregivers, some of whom were beneficial, while others - not so much. After those hands, we either fall or walk into the hands of our peers, which can be even more influential to our good, or, perhaps far too often, to our harm.

Many of us can look back on our childhood and see that some of the agendas and instincts we developed in order to get what we wanted when we wanted it, and to protect ourselves from further wounding are no longer helpful. We may have learned to be agreeable at all costs, or to stand our ground whether we are right or wrong. We may have learned to demand what we wanted when we wanted it, or the opposite, to never ask for anything. My point is that no matter how functional or protective these agendas and instincts were and are, they can form into a hardened crust of resistance to God who desires to conform us to the image of His Son.

Referring back to Romans 12:2, it is fine for Paul to say that we need to be transformed by the renewing of our minds, but even with the Bible and the Holy Spirit, that seems difficult to do on our own as individual believers. What we also need is a family of believers who provide love, support, fellowship, encouragement, and if necessary, accountability. God provides this family, which is His Son's body, the Church, where believers and nonbelievers can find a healthy family, and where they can experience what may have been missing in childhood. In the next Section we will look at His Church.

Questions

1) Do you get to make mistakes and still be loved and accepted by God? Why might that be difficult for you to believe?

2) What does "Be still and know I am God" feel like for you? What is your experience when doing this?

3) What would it be like for you to climb onto God's altar everyday with everything you are, including anything about you that has been deformed to the "pattern of this world," and present it all to Him? Rest assured, nothing you bring to God's altar will be a surprise to Him.

SECTION 4

His Church

It is comforting to wear Jesus as our only yoke, and to know that He wants us to experience a personal relationship with Him that is as intimate as a branch is with its vine. It is also comforting that He gives us the Holy Spirit to fill and flow through us as we do the works that God has prepared in advance for us to do. We are also comforted in knowing that each of us is not a single lonely branch wandering aimlessly on the ground because Jesus has made us members of His body, the Church. God's provision for us is complete in that he provides a relationship with our Savior, an advocate who is the Holy Spirit, and a family of believers who are His Son's body.

CHAPTER 11

His Body

Jesus' love for His Church is so fiercely consuming that He gave himself up for her, cleanses and washes her, and will present her to himself radiant without stain, wrinkle, or blemish. (based on Ephesians 5:25-33) As such, it matters to Him what we do in and through His Church, and how we stay in relationship with one another. It also matters to a watching world that is waiting to experience His love through us.

Since the Church is a physical presence of the body of Jesus in the world, nonbelievers will know of Him and experience His love by knowing and experiencing life with the members of His Church. Without our love and the ministry of the Holy Spirit, Jesus will live only as a man in history, and the Bible will live only as a book on a shelf – just another collection of stories and poems competing for readers of fantasy, adventure, or science fiction.

Constrained

Jesus has deliberately constrained much of Himself in us, His body, by making us His legs to go out into the world, and His arms and hands to minister to those who are in need. As much as He would like to physically feed starving children, if we do not, they starve. As much as He would like to physically comfort those who mourn, if we do not, they remain alone in their suffering. It is not that all starving children and all of those who mourn will not be fed or comforted, because just as Jesus told a man in Matthew 8:22, "Follow me, and let the dead bury their own dead," the "dead" will continue to feed and comfort at least some of their own. The only questions are, "Who will be glorified?" and "Who will be rebuked for the dead having to feed and comfort their own?" Of course, those who are hungry and mourn could not care less from whose hands they are fed or in whose arms they are comforted. Little do they know that the testimony of their lives will be very important one day.

Jesus intends that those who are hungry or mourn will receive food and comfort from Him through the members of His body whose hearts have been transformed and whose minds are being renewed. Not only will those who hunger and mourn have their physical and emotional needs met, they will also hear of, and possibly receive Jesus Himself. When they do, He also will provide for their spiritual life as they enter into a vine and branch relationship with Him, and a branch and branch relationship with other Christians.

An Imperfect Body

The body of Christ is always an imperfect work in progress. His Church is not quite radiant yet, and still needs some cleansing as it struggles to grow corporately with members who at the same time are also struggling to grow individually. What complicates the growth of His body is that members continually leave to be with Him, while new members join and must learn the same spiritual lessons their predecessors had to learn.

People who do not know Jesus are watching and waiting for His Church to reach out to them. As such, Jesus needs the Church of each generation to grow and actively reach out to those who are alive during its generation. Past accomplishments are laudable, but today's hungry cannot re-feast on yesterday's meals.

For the remainder of this section, when I use the terms *body* and *Church* I am speaking spiritually as opposed to a local expression of His body, which I will refer to as a *congregation*. The reason for this distinction is that speaking of His body or the Church can sound spiritual, yet remain distant and sterile when it comes to serving as the body of Jesus in a community. As such, congregations are the legs, arms, and hands of Jesus that He uses to reach out locally to both believers and nonbelievers in need.

It is unsettling to imagine a local congregation with Jesus as its head that does not reach out to its local generation. Unfortunately, some congregations do not *reach out*, and are content to only *reach in*, to and for themselves. These congregations cease to be the body of Jesus with the purpose of living His love to the world, and become a Club whose members are concerned primarily with maintaining the standards and comfort of the Club. I will refer to this Christ-decorated facade as a Club of christ (lowercase "c" intended). When these Clubs fail to allow Jesus to live through them, they are consigned to studying dead Christians, and piously impersonating Jesus to a watching and rarely fooled world.

As I describe the differences between a healthy congregation and a healthy Club of christ, it is important to understand that all congregations fall somewhere between these two extremes. Every congregation evolves over time in either direction as its members continually face the challenge of what it means to be the local body of Jesus in their community. As you look for a congregation to join, it will be helpful to keep the following characteristics in mind.

Characteristics of a Healthy Congregation

1) A healthy congregation is organized with Jesus as its head, and pastors as servant leaders. It consists of members who are connected first individually to Jesus as their head, and second to one another as members of His local body.

2) A healthy congregation accepts its unique distinctions such as type of music and order of worship as no more than preferences that are subject to the authority of Jesus and the moving of the Holy Spirit, as long as all are done in order with reverence to God.

3) A healthy congregation understands that fellow believers can have differing preferences and still be members of the body of Christ. Those who choose to leave the congregation for another, do so with the assistance and pastoral care of its leaders, and are as blessed when leaving as they are when staying.

4) A healthy congregation is an oasis of hope consisting of imperfect believers whose extended arms hold and comfort both

members and non-members who are weary, burdened, and in need of rest.

5) A healthy congregation understands and practices disciplines of grace such as studying the Bible, praying, and fasting when able. These disciplined activities are *responses* to God's grace, not *requirements* for His acceptance.

6) A healthy congregation is a safe place for people to be honest about their struggles with spiritual growth, and to be open about their wounds and personal pain.

7) A healthy congregation views the Bible as a record of God's interactions with mankind in the past, which is to be studied and discussed to provide guidance for today's decisions. Members look to the Holy Spirit to direct and empower them as they allow Jesus to live and work through them daily. They understand that it is Jesus who is responsible for their activities as they take Him as their yoke, and remain in a vine and branch relationship with Him.

8) A healthy congregation emphasizes a *centered* approach to the continual conformation of its members to the image of Jesus. As such, a member who is *closer,* for the lack of a better word, in his or her relationship with Jesus and personal walk with Him, and is *drifting away,* raises even more concern than someone who is *further away* and continuing to move *closer.* The former needs urgent and loving reconnection, while the latter needs consistent and loving encouragement.

9) A healthy congregation focuses on repentance and relationship with Jesus as the basis for belonging, and its members lovingly lift one another up to the hope that He has placed in each of them. Salvation and the ministry of the Holy Spirit are the only requirements for members to serve others in their congregation with the personal and spiritual gifts that God has given them.

10) A healthy congregation is a welcoming body that embraces people at all phases of their spiritual journey. It provides love and compassion in the context of discernment, and administers discipline when necessary.

Unfortunately, congregations do not always start out or remain healthy because they are an imperfect family made up of imperfect people. In addition, congregations are led by imperfect leaders who themselves are at varying stages of personal growth and spiritual health. This is why each member of a congregation needs his or her own vine and branch relationship with Jesus so He can live His life through them both individually and corporately.

Characteristics of a "Healthy" Club of christ

As I mentioned previously, all congregations fall somewhere between what I have just described as a healthy congregation, and the following description of a healthy Club of christ.

1) A healthy Club of christ has leaders who control the activities of the Club, and who perceive themselves as Executive Officers, or worse yet, owners of the Club. They surround themselves with like-minded people to prevent the emergence of differing views and personal accountability.

2) Members of a healthy Club of christ are first committed to one another as a clan under the banner of the Club. The Club functions as a closed-in compound of conformity whose characteristics differ minimally from other secular clubs and organizations.

3) Members of a healthy Club of christ are offended when people decide to leave, and often label them as "church hoppers," or accuse them of "looking for the perfect church." Of course, if they ate repeatedly at the same restaurant, and always left feeling hungry and they continued to lose weight, they would hopefully find somewhere else to eat. Imagine the chef scolding them by saying, "You are just looking for the perfect restaurant," or "You should only be coming to my restaurant to cook and serve tables for me and my patrons, not eat for yourselves."

4) A healthy Club of christ focuses on extra-biblical rules that are additional yokes for its members to wear. The Club's extended arms toward members and non-members hold *hoops of works* through which everyone must jump in order to join and remain.

5) A healthy Club of christ understands and practices disciplines

such as studying the Bible, praying, and fasting when able as *requirements* to be achieved in order to be accepted by God.

6) A healthy Club of christ reinforces a *façade* of spiritual growth, because honesty about one's spiritual struggles, wounds, and personal pain is often responded to with discomfort, disapproval, and avoidance. As far too many Christian authors have noted, Christianity is the one army that shoots its wounded.

7) A healthy Club of christ views the Bible as a record of God's interactions with mankind in the past, which are to be studied and discussed to provide guidance for today's decision making. The Club treats the Holy Spirit as a figurehead dignitary whose influence in the Club's day-to-day activities is minimally acknowledged. They see Jesus as someone to work for in order to win His approval.

8) A healthy Club of christ focuses on a *bounded* rather than a *centered* approach to belonging, which emphasizes rules and standards for inclusion that serve primarily to establish and maintain the Club's brand.

9) A healthy Club of christ often requires Christians to be on the Club's roster before they are permitted to use their personal and spiritual gifts in the Club. This requirement is often promoted by leaders who say a roster is necessary for them to know for whom they are responsible, and who is qualified to serve. This reliance on a roster reveals a deeper ignorance and poses a serious threat.

> The deeper ignorance is that pastors have an ongoing responsibility for every person who comes through the church door, saved or not, on the roster or not. Otherwise, a "non-member" could be as disruptive as he or she pleases with the pastor not having the authority or responsibility for asking the person to refrain or leave. The serious threat is that no membership class or slot on a roster validates someone's ability or suitability to serve, nor does it prevent someone who fulfills the requirements of the roster from becoming a predator of the lambs or sheep.

The qualifications for serving within a congregation are found in the Bible, and come from Jesus and the ministry of the Holy Spirit alone, not from attending a membership class and signing a form. And when problems arise, spiritually applied church discipline with discernment in the power of the Holy Spirit is adequate for protecting a congregation and the name of Jesus before a watching world. Requiring someone to be on a roster in order to serve within a congregation is adding man's law to grace, which is not a yoke made of Jesus.

Of course, membership rosters are fine for congregations who prefer to use that form of governing for managing organizational issues such as approving budgets, administering church assets, or making personnel decisions. Obviously, no one wants a situation in which 500 people masquerading as *new members* show up at a business meeting to replace a pastor or to vote on the sale of church property.

10) A healthy Club of christ is highly selective about who is welcome to join and who is allowed to remain. I have heard it taught that churches should guard their front door by raising their standards for joining, and be more willing to exclude those who were not *sufficiently committed* by opening the back door and encouraging them to leave. The reason for this strategy was that a church should maintain its *holy separation from the world*. The biblical support for this stance was Matthew 7:14, " But small is the gate and narrow the road that leads to life, and only a few find it." I understand that the road to life is narrow, but is it possible that the pew in the Club is narrower? This begs the questions, "Just how wide is the blood of Christ?" and "How conformed to the image of Jesus does someone already need to be before being allowed to enter through the Club's front door?"

If a healthy Club of christ wants a guard at the front door, it had better not ask Jesus to do it because He has a nasty habit of welcoming prostitutes and tax collectors, and me, as well as people who think the front door of His Church needs guarding.

If Jesus is not qualified to guard the front door to keep the right people out, who is? Not I or anyone I have ever known. Think for a moment of a guard who must decide which person can or cannot enter in the same way that admittance to an upscale night club is controlled. Now picture the guard looking down at someone and saying, "No. You are not conformed enough to the image of Jesus." Do you want to be the one who then finds himself face-to-face with Jesus when He asks, "How dare you turn away someone just like you for whom I suffered, died, and rose again?"

If you think this section on a healthy Club of christ sounds harsh, recall what Jesus did to the money changers in the temple.

> [13] When it was almost time for the Jewish Passover, Jesus went up to Jerusalem. [14] In the temple courts he found people selling cattle, sheep and doves, and others sitting at tables exchanging money. [15] So he made a whip out of cords, and drove all from the temple courts, both sheep and cattle; he scattered the coins of the money changers and overturned their tables. [16] To those who sold doves he said, "Get these out of here! Stop turning my Father's house into a market!" [17] His disciples remembered that it is written: "Zeal for your house will consume me." (John 2:13-17)

If Jesus' zeal was this great towards those who were turning His "Father's house into a market!" think about how He will respond to those who are using His name to edify and serve themselves and are turning His body into a Club, or even worse, are turning His back on those in need. For them, a mere whip would be a welcomed relief.

Guarding a Congregation

Every congregation experiences the tension between the pull of the culture in which it finds itself and the drawing of the Holy Spirit. For this reason, the pressure on a congregation to deform to its culture is often as insidious as it is pervasive, which is why guarding a congregation is everyone's responsibility. If spiritual attacks are as deadly as the Bible claims, the entire congregation should be vigilant at all times. Everyone needs to be on guard against predators and the eroding destruction of being deformed to the "pattern of this world," rather than being conformed to the image of Jesus. One of the greatest threats to a congregation is self-serving leaders who want to take it captive.

Self-Serving Leaders and Captive Congregations

Remaining in a vine and branch relationship with Jesus is difficult work and often confusing, so congregations can easily become deceived into following a leader's simplified list of *vine-like* rules. This vulnerability of Christians for following manmade rules is not lost on self-serving leaders. These leaders learn that it is easier to control committed and energetic followers if you can get them to obey a set of rules that use spiritual sounding words, but are devoid of the life of Christ and the power of the Holy Spirit. Followers who succumb to this deception often become branches from the leader's vine with 1) a flow of life that is not from Jesus, 2) a feeling of belonging that is not in His body, and 3) a sense of power that is not from the Holy Spirit.

Being a servant of a self-serving leader eventually becomes debilitating because it is like a horse eating poor quality hay; its stomach feels full while its body continues to waste away. Rather than being a living sacrifice on God's altar, these servants become a living sacrifice on their leader's table. They are led to believe they are needed, but in reality, the leader is *kneading* them into a dough for baking in his own image to be consumed for his own purposes. Self-serving leaders become masters at siphoning life from a follower's true vine and branch relationship with Jesus, or worse, they provide a counterfeit faith that intercepts and aborts a potential believer's God-initiated drawing to Himself.

A common technique of self-serving leaders is to isolate their followers from family and non-following friends in the same way that child abusers isolate their victims. If this happens to you, your temple of the Holy Spirit will at best be shared with another, or much worse, may never have been the Holy Spirit's at all. I would not like to be a self-serving leader who God finds in possession of His hijacked children.

Questions

1) What traits of a healthy congregation or a Club of christ characterize your congregation? Remember, every congregation of believers is somewhere between the two extremes that I described.

2) What traits of a healthy congregation or a Club of christ characterize your own walk with Jesus?

3) How would you know you were serving a self-serving leader?

4) What wisdom regarding self-serving leaders can you pass on to a new believer? This wisdom is not gossip if it is true and your intent is to protect the body of Christ.

CHAPTER 12

Shrewd and Innocent, or Naïve

When Jesus sent His disciples out as "sheep among wolves," He told them to be "as shrewd as snakes and as innocent as doves" (Matthew 10:16). Jesus was warning His disciples about how they needed to respond to the difficult people they would encounter.

A problem many Christians have is they are naïve sheep among shrewd wolves. They seem to think *naïve ignorance* is a spiritual state, and *wishful thinking* is a trusting faith. Christians are not meant to remain naïve or wishful. Jesus tells us in Matthew to take His yoke and learn from Him, and the Apostle Paul tells us in Ephesians to put on the full armor of God. If you choose not to wear Jesus as your only yoke, and not to put on all of God's armor, you risk not only your own well-being, but also the well-being of others who are depending on you to accomplish the works that God has prepared in advance for you to do.

Randi

We live near a winery that hosts weddings. During the spring and summer, some couples like the idea of white doves being released at the end of the ceremony. As it turns out, white pigeons look a whole lot like white doves and, according to one caterer, can be trained to return to their handler. I have no idea if this was the case, but one day a *white dove-alike* started roosting on the gutter of our garage. Our oldest daughter decided the bird was a "she," and named her Randi.

Randi brought us joy each night as we sat in the driveway. In addition to being beautiful, she flew gracefully low to the ground in and among the trees. Each night we would check on her before going to bed and each morning she would be gone doing whatever she needed to do that day.

One windy afternoon I was driving down our street and as I got closer to our home I noticed that our neighbor's trash must have blown over because white packing peanuts were scattered across their yard. When I reached our driveway I realized that what I was seeing was white feathers. I parked my car and started walking over to investigate, and that is when I saw a hawk standing over Randi's body eating its meal.

I had seen this hawk before and thought it was probably the reason that Randi always flew low to the ground in and among the trees. But then again, Randi may not have known what a hawk was, or what it was capable of doing to her. Whichever it was, she knew now. As I walked closer I could feel myself getting angry that a beautiful part of our lives had been destroyed, and how much sadness it would bring my wife and our daughters. But, at the same time I knew this hawk was just doing what hawks do. It was not personal; it was appetite. At about that time, the hawk crouched and thrust itself into the air with Randi's lifeless body clutched in its talons. It flew off gracefully low to the ground in and among the trees. Randi the pigeon was *as innocent as a dove*, and had failed fatally to be *as shrewd as a hawk.*

Snakes, Hawks, and Wolves

You will encounter many snakes, hawks, and wolves as you drive your cart along your path. Effectively guarding yourself, your family, and your congregation requires that you be intentional when it comes to doing the spiritual and mental work of acquiring wisdom and developing discernment. Failing to do this work, or to take spiritual threats seriously will result in the unnecessary wounding of believers, and the feeding of snakes, hawks, and wolves. Recall that God predestined us to be conformed to the image of His Son, not the shape of snake scat, hawk droppings, or wolf dung.

Effectively guarding yourself, your family, and your congregation also requires faith, wisdom, and strength, not timidity, ignorance, and weakness. As the Apostle Paul wrote to Timothy, "For the Spirit God gave us does not make us timid, but gives us power, love, and self-discipline" (2 Timothy 1:7). Paul spoke with this same power, love, and self-discipline when he confronted the Galatians about those who wanted to require Christian males to be circumcised as evidence of their faith. His suggestion that they "emasculate themselves" was certainly not a timid statement. It seems clear that this battle over circumcision was critical because circumcision was being required as yet another *yoke of the law* that was not made of Jesus and His grace.

But what about Jesus' command to turn the other cheek? Turning the other cheek should always be done in the context of power, love, and self-discipline. Can you imagine a lamb all decked out in the full armor of God who then offers his throat to wolves? That is exactly what Jesus did on the cross. It takes wisdom and discernment from the Holy Spirit to know when, during a spiritual battle, to stand firm in faith, wisdom, and strength, and turn the other cheek in meekness and humility, or when to stand firm in faith, wisdom, and strength, and swing the sword of the Spirit as a conquering warrior.

Questions

1) What snakes, hawks, or wolves have you survived? Where does the outcome of their attacks rank on a scale from you living with anger and bitterness to you living with wisdom and forgiveness?

2) What lessons on becoming wise and remaining innocent have you learned from the attacks of others? What wisdom can you pass on to your fellow believers? Hopefully, they will listen.

SECTION 5

You

Knowing that God's will is to conform you to the image of His Son, Jesus, who is your yoke, you have a choice to continually make as you confront the difficulties in your life along with the snakes, hawks, and wolves.

CHAPTER 13

Knowing What You Know Now

Let's go back in time to just before Adam was created and the earth was waiting to be populated. Now imagine that you are in a room, a very large room, with row after row of seats. You are sitting in your row some distance from the front. You can see two people in the first row and somehow you know they are Adam and Eve. You also see their children in the second row. As the rows of people get closer to yours, most of them get wider. That is when you realize that everyone in the room represents the generations of believers who will populate the earth; one row for each generation. Then you become curious about your own row.

You look to your left and to your right and you think, "These are the people who will be the body of Jesus with me." Others in your row are looking around and some are looking at you. You can tell they are coming to the same conclusion, and you begin talking with one another. The excitement builds with the anticipation that your row and everyone else in the room will be together again when Jesus establishes His eternal kingdom. The talking quickly turns to silence when Jesus appears at the front of the room. He speaks and begins with what everyone has just realized.

"All of you are my body throughout your appointed generation."

Relief spreads across the room, but that feeling changes quickly as

He looks directly at the front row and continues.

"Some of you will have a family in which one child kills another. Others of you will form a great nation that will eventually be enslaved. Many of you will long for my coming, while others of you prophesy the event, and still others of you in the back row will see it come to pass. As different as all of you are and as much as you will do over the generations, it is the faith I give you and my commitment to never let go of you that will bring you back here. For me, everything is already finished, though for you it is yet to unfold."

He then looks over at a group of His chosen disciples and says,

"I will give you authority in your generation to drive out demons and impure spirits, heal the sick, cleanse those who have leprosy, and raise the dead. As you go out into the world proclaim this message: 'The kingdom of heaven has come near.' Freely you will receive; freely give. I want you to feed those who are hungry and comfort those who mourn. Bear one another's burdens and love one another in the same way I love you, and teach others to do the same.

"I will send you out like sheep among wolves. Therefore be as shrewd as snakes and as innocent as doves. Be on your guard; some of you will be handed over to the local councils and be flogged in the synagogues. On my account you will be brought before governors and kings as witnesses to them and to the Gentiles. But when they arrest you, do not worry about what to say or how to say it. At that time you will be given what to say, for it will not be you speaking, but the Spirit of your Father speaking through you."

As Jesus pauses you think, "Those disciples are going to have it rough." Then He looks out over the rest of the room.

"I am sending all of you out in the same way. Some of you will suffer from the same persecution they will and I have. Some of you will be starving and pray for food, and I will send someone to feed you, while others of you will die with only your prayer on your lips. Some of you will pray for healing and I will heal you, while others of you will pray and remain sick. Many of you will watch your loved ones be healed or remain sick as well.

"Some of you will pray for protection and I will protect you, while others of you will be abused, raped, or murdered, and when this is happening you will call out to me and I will not make it stop. Some of you will be those abusers, rapists, and murderers before you finally turn to me.

"Some of you will pray to have children and you will receive them, while others of you will miscarry or be unable to conceive. Some of you will have children who bring you immeasurable joy, while others of you will have children who cause you unfathomable sorrow. Some of you will have children you watch die, while others of you will not be born. For those of you who will be aborted, some of you will be aborted by one of my other children who is sitting with you in this room.

"Some of you will be born into poverty or war surrounded by death with no means of escape, while others of you will be born into luxury with no desire left unmet. Give me your desires and your lack of desire, and I will shape them both into my desires for you and my desires for others that will be met through you. Yield your strength and weakness and riches and poverty to me, and whatever you lose on the earth for my sake will be more than restored to you.

"Many of you will seek the perfect combination of prayer and works to release my blessings or prevent your suffering. There is no secret combination to my will, though many deceivers will try to convince you otherwise. There are no rituals to predict or control my actions. There is only my will and my grace and my love and my blood for you, and the promise that when I bring the ages to an end, you will know and understand as fully as you are known and understood by me. Your hope needs to be in me, not in what you think I will do for you.

"Look around and see my body. You are my body with feet and arms and hands that will go to and reach out to your generation in need. You will be hated by some and always loved by me. At times you will even hate one another, but remember that all of you are brothers and sisters, and my bride whom I will present spotless without blemish. Throughout your living and blessing and giving and sinning and suffering and dying I am with you, and I have already died and overcome death for you.

"As you are conformed to my image you will learn much about yourselves that will cause you great distress, but understand that I am not surprised because I already know you. When you come to me I will receive all that you are, including all that you have done and all that you will do. My all-knowing grace is sufficient for you as well as for those you help and those you harm. My ways and my grace and my purposes are greater than you can understand until we are back together again. All of your wounds will be healed and all of your desires that remain will be fulfilled.

"Your lives will be difficult because the world will fall. Your lives will be difficult because of the spiritual war you are entering. Your lives will be difficult because I will be hated. But be of good cheer for I have overcome the world."

With His last statement, the other people in the room fade away. You notice that He is no longer in the front of the room and is now standing directly in front of you. You are alone – with Him. The only difference is that the time is now, right here, right now as you are reading this book. He asks you,

> "Knowing what you know now, and having experienced all that you have in your life, and knowing what can happen, will you trust me? Will you trust me with your pain and your loss and your joys and your hopes? I promise that when you and I are united again with all of your brothers and sisters, you will understand my purposes and your pain. So I ask you again, knowing what you know now, having experienced all that you have in your life, and knowing what can happen, will you trust me?"

If your answer is "No," He still loves you and will wait patiently until you are ready. He will not lose anyone whom the Father has given Him. If your answer is "Yes," then come to Him daily and take Him as your only yoke. You will learn from Him and find rest for your soul.

SECTION 6

Helping Others

In the first half of this book I proposed that Jesus is our personal yoke who does not add unnecessary weight or an additional burden. We also have a oneness and separateness relationship with Him that he compares to that of a vine and its branches.

In addition, I described how we learned to drive our cart from parents, caregivers, and peers during childhood, and that much of what we believe about ourselves and the agendas we developed for self-protection and getting what we want when we want it may no longer be helpful once we become a temple of the Holy Spirit.

I also pointed out that taking care of our ox/body is our responsibility in order to give more of our *one mores* to others such as a kind word, a song, or wisdom, and to live long enough to experience our *not yets*, which have not yet happened. I addressed that some circumstances cannot be changed, and that our battle for healing, restoration, and wholeness benefits both ourselves and those with whom we share our life and hard won wisdom.

I also emphasized that we are all on the same path of being conformed to the image of Jesus, and each of us is a unique expression of that image. Truly spiritual battles will occur on our path, and we can only prevail if we yield to the power of the Holy Spirit. Ultimately, this yielding begins with presenting ourselves daily as a living sacrifice to God who works in us to complete the works He has prepared in advance for us to do.

To help us on our journey, God has placed us in the body of His Son, the Church, which is our spiritual family. His body has a local expression, which I refer to as a congregation that we can serve and rely on as we reach out to our own generation in need.

And finally, throughout our journey we will be confronted by many circumstances and outcomes that can only be endured and conquered by faith that God's grace, mercy, and justice are sufficient for us. Jesus has already prevailed, though our day-to-day experience of His victory is yet to unfold. As such, each day of faith is a continued commitment to Jesus as we live out our own calling of Matthew Chapter 10.

The Remainder of This Book

Now that we know who we are in Christ, the power of the Holy Spirit in us, and that we are each on a unique journey to be conformed to the image of Jesus, the remainder of this book is about helping people, and learning to be "as shrewd as snakes" while remaining "as innocent as doves." Recalling what happened to Randi the pigeon, what follows is more specifically about how to prevent you and others from being *eaten by a hawk*.

As I mentioned in the Introduction, I will be sharing many concepts from biblical counseling that help explain why our interactions with one another can be difficult. Unfortunately, there is no way I can do each topic justice, so I encourage you to read other sources for more thorough discussions. Unfortunately, in your reading you will notice that the definitions of many of these concepts have shifted over the years and also differ in their use among authors. As such, I encourage you to focus on the concepts themselves and not the specific labels used by a particular author.

What I present in this book is not merely for your intellectual understanding. Your path is difficult and dangerous, and you have an enemy who may take your spiritual life more seriously than you do. For that matter, he wants to *take* your spiritual life – period.

Four Possible Points of Concern

First, what I write is not true of all people all of the time. The vast majority of people are wonderful and loving until they are not. You can be completely relaxed and trusting around all of them until you have what they want when they want it. I was asked by a student why friends were always the ones who "stabbed her in the back." I thought for a moment and said, "Probably because they are the only ones you let back there." Obviously, this does not mean that all friends or people you are trying to help will take advantage of you, just do not be surprised when someone does.

Second, being "as shrewd as snakes" does not mean you have to be a snake. Remember, Jesus also told his disciples to be "as innocent as doves." You can learn to understand poisonous snakes well enough to handle them safely without becoming one.

Third, nothing I write is meant to degrade or demean anyone in any way. The material that follows is meant to help you love others more deeply and effectively by giving you a better understanding of their wounds and defenses for preventing further pain, along with their motivations and strategies for getting what they want when they want it. Remember, snakes are just being snakes, hawks are just being hawks, and wolves are just being wolves. The problem is that a single snake, hawk, or wolf can do a lot of damage. You should also keep in mind that all of us have probably been labeled as a snake, hawk, or wolf by someone, justified or not.

Fourth, you do not have to believe a thing I write, and you do not have to put in the mental and spiritual effort to acquire wisdom. You can continue on your path through life just as you are in the same way that Randi continued to fly gracefully low to the ground in and among the trees. Hawks are patient and only kill when hungry. Satan on the other hand has an insatiable appetite and kills for the pure joy of it.

Acquiring Wisdom

Acquiring wisdom can be as simple as listening to others who have more experience than you. Proverbs 12:15 says, "The way of fools seems right to them, but the wise listen to advice." I learned this lesson the hard way when I was fresh out of veterinary college and a new client came in with her cat that had a bite wound on its back.

I entered the examination room and was greeted by a young woman who appeared to be in her early fifties. She wore a business suit and had a pleasant smile. After examining her cat I told her I would be right back. I returned with a vial of tablets. When I told her to give one tablet twice a day until they were gone, she said, "I'm sorry, that will not do because he will not take pills." I told her that giving pills was not that difficult to which she replied, "He will not take a pill. We have tried before." That is when my stupid rose up in me and I said, "Any cat can be pilled."

The woman was wiser and shrewder than any young veterinarian, and she knew how to remain innocent. As I looked at her I noticed the corners of her mouth extend ever so slightly outward and upward. I also saw a sparkle begin to form in her eyes as she said, "Would you mind giving him the first one?" "I'll be glad to," I replied, eager to demonstrate my skill. I was soon to find out that what I had noticed about the corners of her mouth and eyes could best be described as, "The wry smile of one who knows, and the anticipatory gleam of what one will see."

A few minutes later the cat was on the floor in the corner panting rapidly, and I was standing by the door panting almost as rapidly. There were three tablets strewn between us in varying states of salivary dissolve. The only effort my client made during the entire ordeal was to keep from laughing. If her cat had not been declawed on the front feet he would have shredded me into a cheerleader's pompom. As it was, I looked like I had played the first half of a basketball game in my street clothes. I finally looked up at her and said, "Ma'am, I owe you a sincere apology. I think we should try a liquid." She replied pleasantly, "I think that would be an excellent idea." I left the room, came back, and gave the first dose without incident.

People can be a lot like that cat and it helps to have wisdom and insight from others on how to work with them. You are welcome to whatever wisdom and insight is found on these pages, and free to ignore the rest. You may even decide to ignore it all, but be warned, there are people out there who play for keeps and they are not declawed. They believe what is theirs is theirs, and what is yours is negotiable, including your hopes and dreams.

Questions

1) Why can learning wisdom from others be difficult?

2) What wisdom from others have you acted on, and are glad you did?

3) What wisdom from others do you wish you had responded to? Why was it difficult for you to receive their wisdom?

CHAPTER 14

Relationships in General

In this chapter and several that follow I will explain many concepts that counselors are taught in order to be *as wise as clients*. This will be helpful to you because these clients who usually visit their counselor once or twice a week are the very same people you and I encounter all day every day. To be absolutely honest, they are also the same people you and I *are* all day every day. As such, this book is not only written to you and me, it is also written about you and me. As you read further, you may well say to yourself, "So that's what they have been pulling on me," or perhaps, "So that is what I have been pulling on them." In either case, remember that God's grace is sufficient for all of us, and your response to others based on what you learn in this book should embody the same grace as well.

Give and Receive

You have probably heard that healthy relationships are "give and take." I prefer the phrase "give and receive" in that one person gives and the other receives what is offered. People who "take" from a relationship often end up taking more than what the giver was willing to give, even though the giver may not resist. This type of relationship is more characteristic of a parasite robbing life from its host.

Christians often struggle with how much to give of themselves. The balance is to give only what you intend to give. Anything beyond that will leave you feeling drained and abused, which can only occur with your permission, the result of your naïveté, or perhaps a willingness or psychological need to be abused. While I am not saying how much you should give in a relationship, I am saying that what you give needs to be intentional for it to be a gift.

Abuse in the area of giving and receiving can be a reenactment of childhood wounds for those whose needs and desires were not acknowledged, affirmed, and met by parents, caregivers, family members, or peers. For many of these children, acceptance required unconditional submission and servitude. The corrupted substitute for their *give and receive* relationships was *give and give and give and give*.

As with any gift, someone else must be willing to receive. People who are not willing to receive, deny others of the joy of giving, and people who are always giving, deny others of the opportunity to grow in that area.

Questions

1) When have you been in a relationship where you ended up giving more than you intended? Why do you think you did, and should you prevent that from happening again? If so, how?

2) Are you willing to receive from others? Why or why not?

3) How balanced are you in your giving and receiving?

4) Have you ever taken from a relationship more than someone intended to give? If so, why do you think you did and are you content with continuing to do the same to others?

Expectations in a Relationship

A relationship implies an agreement with rules and expectations. For example, countries have specific rules for how drivers of cars will relate to one another. These rules include which side of the road to drive on and what speeds are acceptable. Our personal relationships with others have similar rules, such as how often we meet, what we do, and whether or not we have conversation or one of us talks continuously while the other is a captive audience.

Another example of rules and expectations is among players in a *pickup game* such as basketball or soccer. The players enforce the rules and the rules can vary widely depending upon the mix of players. Sometimes the rule on calling fouls is that the player who thinks he or she *was fouled* is responsible for calling the foul. Other times it is the opposite in that the player who *fouls* is responsible for making the call. This is when expectations and tolerance can be wide-ranging because for some players the rules are the same as for an organized game, while for others the one rule is, "No blood, no foul." Most of the time it only takes a game or two for everyone to get on the same page of that day's rulebook. Problems arise however when a player wants to be untouchable when he has the ball, and a mixed martial arts fighter when his opponent has it. This inconsistent application of the rules, even if sincerely believed by the aggressor, rarely ends well in pickup games, and can cause serious problems in personal relationships.

Unequal Relationships

Many relationships are meant to be unequal in that the roles and expectations are not the same for both people. I have a different set of rules and boundaries for a relationship with a physician than I do with my friends. A physician can do things to me that I am not permitted to do in return, and the legal rules of our relationship are determined by an established code of ethics and standards of care. However, rules for relationships with our family and friends are not so well-defined, nor are they externally enforced by a "code of ethics " or "standards of care," and often are not even mutually agreed upon.

Family Relationships

Relationships with family members differ from pickup games, physicians, and friends in that these other relationships can be temporary, and you can choose to stay or leave. Family relationships, however, are usually not your choice, and family members can show up at anytime for a *pickup game* to be played by their rules if you let them.

Most people do not like to play by hypocritical relationship rules such as, "What is mine is mine and what is yours is negotiable," or "Do as I say, not as I do." Other rules that are particularly toxic to a relationship are, "We don't have any problems," "We don't talk about our problems," and "If you think there is a problem, it is you!" People who find their unequal rules in a relationship personally satisfying often forget that a relationship can die from either end.

A potential problem with family rules can be they are handed down from generation to generation without a second thought. They can be wonderful and spiritually grounded, or as with the partially-shaved dog mentioned earlier, they can be like an embedded rubber band around a family member's neck. These rules are seldom reexamined, and anyone who thinks about doing so may be labeled as disloyal to the family – even by those family members who are gasping for air from the same ever-tightening *family rules rubber band*. Escaping the bondage of a family that lives by these types of rules can be like crabs in a bucket where any freedom-seeker is foiled by the others who keep pulling it back in.

If you do not like the set of rules that a family member, or anyone else for that matter, is using on you, it is your responsibility to *call the foul*. This is often your only chance for freedom because more often than not, the people who should be calling a *relationship foul* on themselves rarely do.

If you are not willing to *make the call* when a family member or friend is abusing your relationship, then take the mental and emotional beating without complaining to others. And if someone is continually complaining to you about another person whom they refuse to confront, you need to decide just how much more of your precious life you are willing to give them.

Questions

1) What relationship rules from others make you uncomfortable? What alternative set of rules would you prefer?

2) What rules do you bring to your relationships? Are you expecting others to conform to your relationship rules in order to win your approval? If so, what do you gain? What do they lose?

Listening to Endless Complaints

Giving your attention to a family member or friend who is stuck in an endless cycle of complaining may seem like a loving act, but to what end? How often does he or she need his or her anxieties about others soothed by your inert and paralyzed attention? Is he or she incorporating you into an ongoing way of coping with life and refusing to take responsibility for his or her own choices? Does this person want his or her real or imagined conflicts resolved, or does he or she only want the attention you are willing to give? Are you helping this person grow mentally, emotionally, and spiritually, or are the two of you only colluding in a mutual dependence?

Mindfill

Just as a landfill is a place where garbage is dumped, you can become a mindfill when you allow yourself to serve as a psychological dumping ground for the frustrations and anxieties of others. The irony is that you only receive a copy of their woes, and they still leave with their originals.

If you are someone's mindfill, even though they depart from you feeling better temporarily, my question to you is, "How do you feel after you have received an infusion of their woes into your mind, and then become a permanent part of your mental experience?" Your sacrifice is the time it took for you to listen, which is gone forever, along with any of the *one mores* you might otherwise have been doing. With your own thoughts, time, and *one mores* at stake, it seems appropriate for you to speak the truth in love, and put an end to the wasteful abuse. In fact, if listening to an attention-seeking mind-filler is not one of your *one mores*, then it probably qualifies as a *not now and tomorrow isn't looking good either*.

Questions

1) Does this section bring anyone to mind? If so, who and why?

2) Are you a mindfill? If so, why do you continue to listen?

3) What benefits do you receive from being a mindfill and listening to someone's continual complaints?

4) What costs do you incur when being a mindfill?

5) What could a healthy relationship with someone who wants to be your mind-filler look and feel like?

6) In what ways can you help someone who continues to complain about the same issues?

7) Are you using others as your mindfill? If so, is that good for you or fair to them?

Get Up and Walk

Jesus was not shy about speaking the truth in love when questioning others about their true desires. Recall what he asked a disabled man who had stayed for thirty-eight years at a pool near the Sheep Gate in Jerusalem.

> 5 1 Some time later, Jesus went up to Jerusalem for one of the Jewish festivals. 2 Now there is in Jerusalem near the Sheep Gate a pool, which in Aramaic is called Bethesda and which is surrounded by five covered colonnades. 3 Here a great number of disabled people used to lie—the blind, the lame, the paralyzed.5 One who was there had been an invalid for thirty-eight years. 6 When Jesus saw him lying there and learned that he had been in this condition for a long time, he asked him, "Do you want to get well?"
>
> 7 "Sir," the invalid replied, "I have no one to help me into the pool when the water is stirred. While I am trying to get in, someone else goes down ahead of me."
>
> 8 Then Jesus said to him, "Get up! Pick up your mat and walk." 9 At once the man was cured; he picked up his mat and walked. (John 5:1-9)

When Jesus asked the man, "Do you want to get well?" that was a valid question because the man had obviously developed a social network of people who enabled him to survive for all of those years. Getting well would change all of that and introduce him to a new life with a new set of rules and responsibilities.

When it comes to you helping others, it is obvious that everyone will not be "cured" immediately upon your command. However, a valid question for you to ask yourself is, "Does this person really want to get well, or am I only being used as an ongoing source of temporary relief?" If you are not sure of the answer, you may need to ask him or her just as directly as Jesus did.

Questions

1) Does this section on willingness to get well bring anyone to mind? If so, are there changes in your relationship that you would like to make? If there are, what are the changes and how can you make them?

2) Can you relate to the man by the pool? Is there an area in your life in which you are afraid to "get up and walk?" If so, roll over and crawl, and Jesus will crawl with you. When you want to stand, He will lift you up. When you walk, He will walk with you. When you run, He will run with you. When you fall, He will lift you up again. If you happen to be terrified to try any of this, it probably means it is worth doing.

CHAPTER 15

Relationships Can Be Painful

Healthy relationships are about making meaningful and hopefully fond memories with others. Of course, some memories are not so fond, which can happen when an imperfect person is in relationship with another imperfect person. A healthy relationship is about trying and succeeding and failing and trying again and committing and failing and asking for forgiveness and receiving forgiveness and committing to try again. Being conformed and remodeled to the image of Jesus is a gradual and error-filled process that requires diligence on our part and considerable patience from those around us. Unfortunately, meaningful relationships can be painful.

During my years as a practicing veterinarian many of my patients were curious as to the taste of my fingers, and only two found out. The second to do so was a Cocker Spaniel.

According to the American Kennel Club, the Cocker Spaniel is "a merry, well-balanced dog that is capable of considerable speed and great endurance." Well, the one that was dropped off by a new client at my office one morning for a rabies vaccination and a heartworm check was pretty low on the merry scale. According to my staff he was fine when they brought him back to the kennel, but seemed to take offense with everyone after being put in a lower cage. When I say "offense" I am referring to something akin to a rattlesnake. Every time I tried to coax him out he would coil up in the corner growling with his stump tail twitching. After several failed attempts at convincing him of my honorable intentions, I decided to use a restraint pole.

A restraint pole is designed to control an animal's head until a muzzle can be applied. It has a loop on one end, and when used properly can be secured enough to not let the animal pull its head out, while also being loose enough to let it breathe comfortably. To my surprise, when I inserted the pole through the slightly open and foot-braced cage door, he calmed down immediately. I placed the loop around his neck and he walked out like we were best friends. I suspect he had contended unsuccessfully with a similar device at a different hospital. I knelt down and easily applied a muzzle. While we remained on the floor and my assistant held him, I drew the blood sample, gave the vaccination, and removed the muzzle so he would be more comfortable. Everyone was relieved that we had completed our objective and that his misconceptions had been resolved.

While I was still kneeling, I turned my head to answer a question from my receptionist and made the mistake of gesturing with my hands. Even though he was four feet away and still on the end of the restraint pole that was being held by my assistant, that not-so-merry, and very "well-balanced dog that is capable of considerable speed and great endurance" lunged and took the thumb of my left hand right out of the air. He obviously did not like the taste because he shook it violently and spit it out.

Perhaps Jesus should have warned me to be *as shrewd as a Cocker Spaniel* because when he bit my thumb, I was *as innocent as a dove.* My patient would likely argue that prior to the bite, I was far from innocent and he was only administering justice, albeit delayed.

People can be a lot like that Cocker Spaniel. You can have some initial difficulties in your relationship with them, and when you think everything is fine – they bite you. Do not be surprised when people bite, especially if you intend to be in ministry as the hands of Jesus. The good news is that I just checked my thumb and it is still there. It hit s th espacebar   onmy   keyboar d just fine.

Given that people bite, and you are a people, you should accept the fact that you bite. Yes, I know, you might claim that you do not bite unless you are bitten, and you have a right to bite because of what has happened to you. Unfortunately, that does not help the thumbs of others.

I can sympathize with my patient. If I was put in a cage and people came at me with a restraint pole, put a muzzle on my face, stuck a needle in me, and stole my blood, I would have bitten all of them. I might even figure out the merits of preemptively biting everyone just to keep them at a safe distance because in his case, growling obviously did not work. My Rule of Thumb would be: *Bite unto others before they have a chance to stick a needle into me.*

Those who protect themselves by preemptively biting in order to prevent a possible involuntary blood donation, eventually have to deal with loneliness and isolation because even the most loving friends and others will get tired of being bitten. For this reason and many others, when you bite someone, try to figure out why, apologize, and do your best not to do it again. Even when you are wronged, you can put on the full armor of God and stand firm without biting back or backbiting. If you need to confront a *biter*, the sword of the Spirit and the truth spoken in love can be effective as long as your self-esteem does not depend on that person's approval and acceptance.

Questions

1) Do you have a person in your life who is similar to that Cocker Spaniel? Several? What strategies can you use to keep from being bitten?

2) If someone keeps "biting" you, why do you keep putting yourself in danger? Is your self-esteem or sense of belonging involved? If so, how will you change your dependence?

3) How would you know if the Holy Spirit was asking you to be shrewd and innocent and keep your thumb at a safe distance, or to be shrewd and innocent and *turn the other thumb*?

Transference

As much as I care for animals, *turning the other thumb* was not going to happen for me and that Cocker Spaniel. The fallout from the incident was not only that I never trusted my patient again, which could easily be justified along with his unwillingness to trust me, rather, I never fully trusted any Cocker Spaniel from then on. I was experiencing transference.

Transference is a concept from counseling that occurs when someone transfers his or her experiences with one person to another. It is the basis for both shrewd wisdom and blind bigotry, and can be a tool used by others to manipulate you or even cause you horrific harm.

Transference can be an essential survival skill. Think about what your life would be like if you had to meet and understand up close and personal everyone who was dangerous and intended you harm. No, it is much preferred to look out ahead on your path and recognize dangerous people based on your previous experiences and the wise counsel you have received from others.

A problem with transference arises, however, when repeated interpersonal wounding results in a person becoming obsessed with preventing further pain. When this happens, his or her transference often labels everyone as dangerous and to be avoided. People who fall into this trap of self-protection, often end up lonely and completely harmed by an empty life. A Christian who is obsessed with preventing further mental or physical trauma by avoiding the risks of meaningful relationships is in danger of becoming a Club of christ with a roster of one and a ministry of none.

Questions

1) What examples of unhealthy transference can you think of?

2) How healthy is your transference towards others?

3) Why could it be difficult to explain your transference to others?

Transference and Winning the Acceptance of Others

When it comes to trust and transference, I should write a bit more about the other Cocker Spaniels who actually were "merry." They would stand there wagging their stump tail wanting me to pet them. They might have been *standing*, but what my transference saw was an *upright coiled Cocker ready to strike*. They might have been *wagging* their tail, but what my transference saw was a *twitching rattle*. Perhaps they sensed my reluctance and could have thought:

"Gee, what's wrong with me?"

"I wagged my tail as nice as I could, and he still rejected me."

"I must have done something wrong. I'm such a bad dog I'm not even worth petting."

"Maybe I can roll over and offer him my belly so he will like me."

Of course a truly "merry, well-balanced dog that is capable of considerable speed and great endurance" would have confidently walked away from me thinking, "What's his problem?"

Have you ever felt like an ignored Cocker Spaniel when trying to win someone's acceptance and approval? My point is that sometimes you are rejected, mistreated, disliked, or ignored, and it has nothing to do with your goodness, badness, desirability, or worth. Any contortions you put yourself through to win their acceptance and approval will only result in a severe psychological cramp.

Of course, the person you are trying to please may offer to be extraordinarily helpful by giving you an unending list of fruitless rules to follow that he or she claims would sufficiently conform you into a sweet enough little dog that you would finally receive your desired pat on the head. I doubt, however, that the image of that sweet little dog looks all that much like the image of Jesus.

Questions

1) Have you ever felt like a Cocker Spaniel wagging its tail in eager anticipation, only to be rejected? If so, how did you interpret the rejection? Was your interpretation accurate? Could there have been other reasons?

2) Are you being conformed into a sweet little dog in order to be accepted by someone? If so, why? Is it worth what it is costing you?

Transference of Trust

While a transference of *mistrust* can cause problems, a transference of *trust* is perhaps even more dangerous because you immediately transfer to one person the trust you have built up over time with another. For example, someone may remind you of a dear friend or favorite relative, so you immediately begin trusting him or her in the same way. A very unusual pet taught me about the potential danger of a transference of trust.

I came home one day and my family greeted me at the door with smiles on their faces. This was rarely good and often expensive. "We bought a pet today!" "Really!?" I said. You see, our home is a Garden of Eden for animals from which no sin will get you expelled. In addition, since I owned a veterinary hospital, our ongoing supply of pets was never in jeopardy. Before I could ask, they said in unison, "It's a rat!" One of them added, "Her name is "Millski." You would think there are enough rats in the world that you would not have to buy one for your home, and why would anyone want to?!!! As it turned out, Millski was a sweet and affectionate pet that we thoroughly enjoyed, though she evoked considerable consternation from our two cats. Millski was not the one who taught me the lesson.

About six months after Millski died, my wife called from our auto mechanic's garage and told me they had found a white rat wondering around and put it in a cardboard box. She said he was nothing but skin and bones, and looked dehydrated. She then followed up with the obvious question, "Should I bring him home?" I drove to the garage, examined him, and agreed that he looked pretty bad and probably would not survive. We decided to bring him home and see what we could do.

It is amazing what a little food and water can do. In less than twenty-four hours he was on his feet – his hind feet. Every time we would get near the box he would stand up on his hind legs, arch his back into the shape of a very un-charmed cobra, and lunge at us. He was no Millski; he was Ratso.

The snake Ratso had found his way into our Garden and he did not want to share it with any other living thing; including us. It was clear that he had endured a difficult life and saw it as his mission to make certain that everyone else's was even more so. We originally thought he must have gotten out of someone's home. It was much more likely that Ratso was put out, and his previous owners were still afraid to leave the safety of their dwelling.

Ratso was inconsolable and untouchable. He certainly was not aquarium-worthy because you would have to get him out to change his bedding and we did not have a rat restraint pole. Even if we did, he probably would have eaten it.

My wife finally came up with the idea of keeping him in a bird cage so the floor could be slid out for cleaning. It took about six months for him to stop lunging at us. His cage bars were not exactly bulging outward from his attacks, but they didn't look all that straight either. After six months he would let my wife gently stroke the back of his head until he got "the look," which meant, "Pull your finger back because his *inner Ratso* is coming out and it's not to play." Our family had a lot of love to give Ratso, but he would receive very little of it. Eventually, he grew several large tumors that drained him of his rage. Just before he died, he was willing to be held.

You will encounter many Millskis and a few Ratsos on your path. If you find yourself trying to help someone who might be a Ratso, you should continually be on guard with discernment, seek the counsel of the Holy Spirit, and get input from other believers who are *as shrewd as Ratsos.*

Questions

1) Who are the Millskis and Ratsos that you have encountered? What has been their effect on you?

2) For the Ratsos you have encountered, what if any warning signs do you recall?

3) Looking back on your relationships with Ratsos, what would you tell a new believer about how to be *as shrewd as a Ratso* while remaining "as innocent as a dove?"

Con Artists and Trusting Transference

Con artists try to leverage your trusting transference. Once they learn something about you, they claim to have the same thing in common. For example, when they find out where you grew up, they claim to have a close friend from that area. When they find out what ministries you value, they claim to have supported the same ones for years, or may even claim to have a relative who served in one of them. Their goal is to gain your trust based on these *claimed experiences* so you will ignore your discernment. If you think "something isn't right" with someone, there is nothing wrong with asking questions to verify his or her integrity. People who are honest have nothing to fear from your scrutiny, and if you uncover one deliberate lie, there are usually many more.

Our responsibility for scrutinizing others in order to protect ourselves and our congregation is similar to what the Apostle Paul wrote about testing prophecies.

> [19] Do not quench the Spirit. [20] Do not treat prophecies with contempt [21] but test them all; hold on to what is good, [22] reject every kind of evil. (1 Thessalonians 5:19-22)

Rejecting every kind of evil means both the obvious evils and the not-so-obvious ones that require discernment. Disabling God's gift of discernment to you and naïvely believing someone's *claims* is not trusting God, rather, it is giving the ultimate gift to someone who intends to harm you, your loved ones, or your congregation.

Further justification for verifying the integrity of others is found in Proverbs 18:17, where it says, "In a lawsuit the first to speak seems right, until someone comes forward and cross-examines." My point is that when it comes to trusting others, Christians should not be reluctant to guard and defend themselves and their congregation by asking questions and continually seeking the Holy Spirit for discernment and guidance. Christians often fail to do this because they do not want to hurt someone's feelings. When I saw the hawk standing over Randi's lifeless body in a landscape of white feathers, it did not seem all that concerned about Randi's feelings; nor will predators of the body of Christ be concerned about yours. My experience has been that the more indignation someone shows when being asked questions, the more needed the questions and their answers are. Ask questions and never go against your discernment, no matter how much your feelings plead otherwise.

Scammed

Ministry is a contact sport and eventually everyone gets scammed. Feel the pain, learn the lesson, and move on with your hard-won and possibly expensive wisdom. Your other option is to waste your future by becoming a bitter curator of your museum of hurts.

I once had an older man bring me his beagle for a rabies vaccination. The man was unshaven, wore tattered clothes, and used a rope for his dog's leash. After vaccinating his dog we walked out to the checkout counter and he pulled a sock filled with coins out of his pocket. I noticed on the medical record that he had another dog for us to vaccinate and he needed to go home to get her. I told him he could wait and pay for both when he came back. Much to my receptionist's surprise, he returned. After vaccinating his second dog, I walked him out to pay and offered to charge him only half price to "help him out." He smiled, nodded his head and thanked me. He reached into a different pocket and pulled out a roll of bills that was much wider than his coin-filled sock. He paused, and then continued smiling as he counted out his half fee. When he looked up and slithered the money across the counter, I gave him my best congratulatory smile and took it without breaking eye contact.

I wish I could say that I learned my lesson from that man and his sock of coins, but I did not. It eventually took a "Christian brother?" whom I had known for a couple of years, and twenty thousand of my dollars for it to finally sink in. As it turns out, being groomed and scammed by someone you think is a Christian is just as expensive financially as when a non-Christian does it, though much more painful spiritually.

Three rules come to mind: First, if a person is turned down for borrowing money by people who know him or her really well such as a mother, father, sibling, or a banker, it is probably not a good idea for you to lend him or her any of yours. Second, if it is too good to be true, it is. And if it really, really, really is too good to be true, it really, really, really is. Third, if you lend money to someone, consider it a gift so if they fail to repay, it will not become a continual source of bitterness.

Questions

1) Have you been scammed? Has the experience(s) resulted in wisdom or bitterness, or some of both?

2) What wisdom from being scammed can you share with others so they can become *as shrewd as whoever scammed you*?

Deceived in a Personal Relationship

A very close friend of mine was asked by her therapist about any early warning signs that she might have seen in her relationship with someone who was so deceitful and ultimately destructive. She answered, "Yes, but I decided to trust him." Her short answer was the result of a long and gradual process.

Few people meet someone for the first time and say, "Excuse me for a moment while I turn off my discernment and decide to trust you." No, it usually begins when a loving, caring, and compassionate person meets someone else who is considerably less so. She or he then listens with empathy to the life stories of the other, which often center around the themes, *I have had a hard life, I am misunderstood,* and *I have never been loved.*

Over time, the stories to my friend contained questionable aspects or recollections, and the details from one story would be inconsistent with those of another. When my friend questioned these details, she was met with his scorn, hurt, and eventually anger for not "listening to the emotional content." My friend learned to not question, and to not break the "trust" he had in her. Her love caused her to ignore the glimpses, and eventually waving yellow flags of warning. When enough lies and deceit had been tolerated, she became incapable of seeing the red flags that others saw. Even 1 Corinthians 13:7 seemed to tell her what her love should do, "It [Love] always protects, always trusts, always hopes, always perseveres." She was conditioned by his grooming to love and trust him to the point that she could no longer hear the Holy Spirit or anyone else.

Deception of this nature is a gradual process that is too long and tedious for the short-term goals of con artists and scammers. The consequences, however, can be lifelong. If you have been deceived in this way, the worst consequence is refusing to love again, protect again, trust again, hope again, and persevere again. God still loves you and remains committed to conforming you to the image of Jesus – who loves. Continue to present yourself as a living sacrifice, and God will use this experience to build wisdom in you and to form you into the lover He intended you to be.

Questions

1) Have you been deceived in a personal relationship? Has the deception(s) resulted in wisdom or bitterness, or some of both?

2) What wisdom from being deceived in this way can you share with others so they can become *as shrewd as whoever deceived you*?

Subconscious Transference

Transference often is not conscious. Have you ever met someone you immediately disliked, or who evoked feelings of angst? I am not talking about discernment, rather, I am talking about a deep visceral reaction that seemed to have little basis in fact. Do not be hasty to present these feelings to God for forgiveness.

Therapists who have these feelings about a client are trained to explore them as a potential source of insight on wounds of their own that may need healing, or any unresolved relationship issues they might have with someone else. Therapists ask themselves questions such as: "When have I felt this way before?" "Are there others from my past or present who trigger me to have similar feelings and react this way?"

My point is that you should explore these feelings in prayer with the Holy Spirit and ask Him for insight as to why you are feeling this way. It often helps to talk with a mature Christian who will be genuinely curious with you about your feelings without condoning them or condemning you. Once you understand your feelings more fully, you will know if anything needs to be healed, or confessed and forgiven.

Jesus does not condemn you for being honest with Him about your feelings, and neither should you condemn yourself for having them. On the other hand, if you find yourself cultivating and caring for your feelings of angst and disgust like a master gardener, you will probably not like their eventual fruit. Even if you do like their fruit, it is safe to say that those who remain around you probably won't.

Projection and Projective Identification

Projection is a psychological maneuver in which someone claims his or her own traits and characteristics, usually the negative ones, are yours, and then reacts towards you accordingly. For example, if a person is arrogant and demanding, he or she accuses you of being arrogant and demanding. If he or she is inconsiderate, rude, or selfish, you are accused of the same.

People who use projection usually do so because they cannot

tolerate their own flaws, and have to find a way to dismiss them from their awareness. Their subconscious strategy is to disown them by projecting them onto others. In essence, the *stink* is still in the room, but it is on someone else's shoes, not theirs. The following story is an illustration of this coping defense.

When I was fourteen years old I thought spending thirty-five cents was a bargain to watch a woman turn into an ape right before my eyes. It was at the Miami County Fair in Troy, Ohio. I and others, all boys, filed into a dimly-lit dank-smelling tent that had three rows of benches. After we got situated, the single light bulb in the tent was turned off and the pounding of recorded drums started. Then a spotlight came on and a woman appeared.

The woman stood there looking very normal in a one piece beige swimming suit. While she looked straight ahead over us as if gazing into the heavens, the narrator told us of her bizarre condition. When he finished speaking, hair started growing out of her skin, and it gradually covered her body. Hair even grew on her face, and the color of her eyes changed from light blue to a deep brown. I was impressed until I noticed that for a split second she had four eyes. The problem was that she had crouched too soon. That is when I realized there was a projector in the back of the tent superimposing the image of a hairy ape onto her. As its bulb got brighter, her "hair" got darker. Eventually she regained her timing with the drums, and whenever her projected ape-ness crouched, she was sure to follow. After a minute or two, the narrator spoke of a miraculous cure, the projector's bulb dimmed, and she returned to her more normal form.

That is exactly what happens when someone uses projection on you. They project themselves onto you in the same way the image of the ape was projected onto the woman, and then they treat you as though you are the ape.

What makes projection so difficult to cope with is that the traits projected onto you often run counter to your character and discernment, though it may be somewhat consistent with your self-doubts or beliefs. If you are a willing or unknowingly naïve canvas for their projections, you may find yourself confused and frustrated, and perhaps even acting uncharacteristically similar to what they are projecting. This response is called *projective identification*, which occurs when you accept their projection as your own image, and act accordingly. You may even begin acting like a hairy and sometimes angry ape that crouches on cue to someone else's music.

When someone projects their undesirable character traits onto you, you can either collude with them and do your own version of their *ape dance*, or you can take a stand for your authentic self and hold on to who God created you to be. What made the ape stunt work was the beige swimming suit that had no character or design of its own, and the woman's willingness to give up her identity and serve as a canvas for the projector's image. If someone is attempting this on you, your only defense is to re-center yourself not in the beam of their light that is being projected onto you, but rather in the beam of God's truth. It helps if you can make an honest assessment of your strengths and weaknesses, so you know which positive and not-so-positive traits are yours, and which are those of your projector. When you do, you can present your entire self as a living sacrifice to God to be conformed to the image of Jesus, and not to someone else who wants to layer his or her own image over yours.

I know people who have had someone use projection on them, and they ended up repenting in prayer and apologizing to the person for traits that were not their own. Interestingly, these people never felt forgiven by God or restored in the relationship, which made perfect sense because the "sin" was not theirs. These types of relationships are based on one person's need to disown his or her own negative traits by projecting them onto someone else. If you find yourself in this situation, your only way out of their "dimly-lit dank-smelling tent" is to transform yourself from scapegoat to *escaped goat*.

Defending against projection or any other psychological assault requires that you know who you really are, and that you establish and defend clear boundaries so the psychological issues of others do not become your own. Defending yourself at a personal level in these situations is consistent with defending the body of Christ at a spiritual level. Any attack that diminishes who you are or who you were created to be is ultimately an attack on God's workmanship. For this reason and many others, it is important for you to set your boundaries, stand firm, and speak the truth in love. We are called to present ourselves as a living sacrifice on God's altar, not on someone else's altar of psychological abuse.

Of course, standing firm in defense of your personal identity and boundaries is difficult if you were never trained to do so by your parents or caregivers, which is why Jesus said to take His yoke and learn from Him. By the way, the day you stop being a projector screen and scapegoat will seem like all hell broke loose. Others are not happy when you refuse to play the role you are assigned in their game, which is to be played by their rules. When you speak the truth in love, you need to hold fast to the hope of a healthy relationship in the future that allows both of you to grow in your relationship with each other, and in your likeness to Jesus.

Questions

1) Can you think of people who have projected their positive or negative traits onto you? If so, what were or are they projecting? Even if the traits are positive, they still are not you.

2) Have you been doing the *ape dance* for someone? What would happen if you stopped, set your boundary, and spoke the truth in love? Is it worth discovering and defending who God meant for you to be?

Relationship Triangles

A triangle in the context of a relationship is when two people unite against a third. This can happen in all areas of life such as relationships with coworkers, friends, members of our family of origin or our family of destination, which is the body of Christ. If you believe everything has a God-intended use, along with a fallen use, you might wonder what God's purpose would be for a relationship triangle. In Matthew 18 Jesus talks about an appropriate use:

> [15] "If your brother or sister sins, go and point out their fault, just between the two of you. If they listen to you, you have won them over. [16] But if they will not listen, take one or two others along, so that 'every matter may be established by the testimony of two or three witnesses.' [17] If they still refuse to listen, tell it to the church; and if they refuse to listen even to the church, treat them as you would a pagan or a tax collector." (Matthew 18:15-17)

In order to take one or two others along, you will first need to tell them about the issue. This gives them the opportunity to provide a wise perspective, and perhaps serve as a buffer to the emotions you are having about the conflict. What could possibly go wrong?

For one thing, there is a problem if you are having a hard time deciding which person to take, so you tell many different people in order to find someone who finally agrees with you. As a general rule, do not tell anyone who cannot have a direct impact on the outcome. By the way, when it comes to talking with others, gossip often masquerades as a *concerned request for prayer*.

Another possible problem could be that you do not accurately represent the other person's position. If you and I have a dispute, there are three realities: what I think happened, what you think happened, and what really happened from God's perspective. Since we are told to speak the truth in love, the question is, do we present our brother or sister's position accurately, truthfully, and in love?

My own experience with a relationship triangle began when I

received a letter from a dog breeder accusing me of being a "horribly unprofessional veterinarian." She proceeded to list the catastrophic and unsupportable predictions that I had made about a puppy she had sold to a new client of mine. Having not included her telephone number, I looked it up and called her. When I identified myself, she was silent. When I told her that I had received her letter, she remained silent. That is when I said that I agreed with her completely. Then came an encouraging, "What?" I told her that if I had said those things, I would be a "horribly unprofessional veterinarian," but what she had written was not what I told my client.

My client had tried to triangulate me against the breeder and neglected to let me in on the plan. Before long the breeder and I were having an enjoyable conversation about dog breeding and several other topics. She decided to give the client a full refund and take the puppy back, not because there was anything wrong with the puppy, but rather, she decided that her puppy "deserved a better home." The point is that if I had not intentionally addressed the manipulative triangle that my client tried to create, the breeder would have believed lies about me. This is not good for business, nor is it good when it happens in the body of Christ

What should you do if someone tries to triangulate you against someone else? I have known Christians who when told an unfavorable report about another person, insist on the three of them meeting together. These Christians refuse to let their congregation be set ablaze by a gossiping *social pyromaniac* who loves to start interpersonal fires of discord. If you adopt this practice of exposure and confrontation, a pleasant benefit is that career social pyromaniacs rarely try it on you a second time.

Questions

1) Identify a triangle in which you were involved. Was it used as God intended or not? What was your role? What was the result?

2) Do you know any *social pyromaniacs*? What is your strategy for protecting your congregation?

3) Are you a *social pyromaniac*? If so, what do you gain from it?

The Altar of Gossip

Have you ever wondered what is so terrible yet savory about gossip, and what God thinks of it? Proverbs 6:16-19 says,

> 16 There are six things the Lord hates,
> seven that are detestable to him:
> 17 haughty eyes,
> a lying tongue,
> hands that shed innocent blood,
> 18 a heart that devises wicked schemes,
> feet that are quick to rush into evil,
> 19 a false witness who pours out lies
> and a person who stirs up conflict
> in the community. (Proverbs 6:16-19)

Evidently, God places the stirring up of conflict in the same category as liars and murderers. This still does not explain, however, why gossip can be so savory to some people.

As strange as it may seem, I think gossiping serves a similar purpose between two people as did sacrificing animals in the Old Testament. A triangle was established among an animal, a worshiper, and God, and the animal was killed so the relationship between the worshiper and God would be restored. Gossiping can serve a similar purpose when two people place the character of another on the altar of their relationship and kill it. The more they devour that person's character, the closer they feel to one another. This may work fine for them until one places the other's character on a different altar for a similar ritualistic meal with someone else. While it may seem poetically just for the eater to become the eaten, this is beneath the body of Christ, not only as an attribute of a congregation, but also literally beneath His body as one more reason He had to be nailed to a cross. If feasting on someone's character seems a bit too graphic, I do not apologize based on the Apostle Paul's admonition to the Galatians.

> 13 You, my brothers and sisters, were called to be free. But do not use your freedom to indulge the flesh; rather, serve one another humbly in love. 14 For the entire law is fulfilled in keeping this one command:

"Love your neighbor as yourself." [15] If you bite and devour each other, watch out or you will be destroyed by each other. (Galatians 5:13-15)

Questions

1) When have others gossiped about you? What was the experience like for you?

2) Do you have the courage to defend the body of Christ against those who gossip? If not, why? Whose approval are you seeking?

Family Strife

When gossiping and devouring of one another happens in a congregation and is not stopped, you always have the option of leaving and joining another. Unfortunately, it is much more difficult to leave one's family of origin when it is plagued with constant strife. Some families devolve into factions that are in continuous conflict, until any one of them is attacked by someone outside the family. Such an attack temporarily unites them into a common defense, while otherwise, they are at one another's throat. What makes being a member of one of these families even more difficult is that from time to time they reorganize themselves into different alliances. For people who are caught in this type of chaotic and psychologically toxic family, their only hope of finding sanity, acceptance, and support for spiritual growth may be with a local congregation. Clubs of christ on the other hand are likely to provide even more chaos, not less. Of course, those people who agree to follow the Club's rules will fit in just fine.

Some Family Pain is Unavoidable the First Time

I saw a friend of mine at a church picnic and noticed he had a considerably blackened left eye. I asked him what happened and he said, "Yeah, my daughter did it." His daughter was all of seven years old so I was intrigued.

He and his daughter were mushroom hunting and they came to a barbed wire fence. He told her he would lift her up over the fence and set her down on the other side. When she pointed out that the fence was "really, really high," my friend assured her that everything would be fine as long as when he lifted her up she would jump high and pull her knees up against her chest higher than she ever had – which she did. As he thrust her into the air with his arms nearing full extension, she jerked her knees up to her chest and at some point in that journey her right knee connected full force with his left eye. He said, "I saw stars and put her right back down. I thought I was going to pass out."

What happened next is why I am telling you this story. She knew he was hurt and immediately hugged him around his waist, and he knew he was hurt and immediately braced himself by holding on to her shoulder. Two people working together in all sincerity, and one got hurt – really hurt.

All of us have or will find ourselves on both sides of a similar story in which someone is hurt either physically, or mentally and emotionally, and the response we choose matters. He could have raged about what she did wrong, rather than admit his plan had an unforeseeable flaw. She could have stood there in silence or even cried about how scared she was and how it was his fault because she only did what he told her to do. No, she chose to hug him and he chose to steady himself by holding on to her shoulder.

At the moment her knee came into contact with his eye, a vivid family memory was set into motion and my friend decided how it would end. These memories start without warning and everyone's mental camera is recording without the possibility of a retake. That is when it really matters if we are experiencing a vine and branch relationship with Jesus. That is when it really matters if we are willing to let his love and grace flow through us. The real choice in this type of situation is which *one mores* you want to have with others. One more *mercy* or one more *condemnation*. One more *as innocent as a dove* or one more *as attacking as a hawk*. One more *hug and being steadied so you don't fall* or one more *bitter memory of lashing out*.

The more he and I talked, I told him that sometimes when something like that happens to me, if I have been focusing my inner world on frustrations and anxieties, or an old wound that I am still nurturing rather than presenting to God for healing, I am like an angry bear being jerked out of his cave. I don't like it when others come out of their inner cave angry at me, and I'm sure others don't like it when I come out at them.

When we encounter these types of situations, what all of us need is a renewed mind that the Apostle Paul talks about in Romans Chapter 12. Let's read it again.

> Therefore, I urge you, brothers and sisters, in view of God's mercy, to offer your bodies as a living sacrifice, holy and pleasing to God – this is your true and proper worship. [2] Do not conform to the pattern of this world,

but be transformed by the renewing of your mind. Then you will be able to test and approve what God's will is—his good, pleasing and perfect will. (Romans 12:1-2)

We are not to present ourselves to an inner world of anger, bitterness, and frustration, only to remain "conformed to the pattern of this world," which causes us to *lash out at others*. Rather, we need to continually present ourselves as a living sacrifice to God so He can transform our minds to the pattern of His will, so He can use us to *reach out to others*.

My friend will be the first to admit that he does not always make the right choice in these situations, and when he doesn't, he is quick to apologize and tries to not let it happen again. That is the best any parent, caregiver, friend, spouse, pastor, relative, fellow member of the body of Christ, or even a stranger can do.

A final observation is that my friend is now *as shrewd as his daughter's right knee*. The next time he lifts her high into the air for any reason, I'm sure she will be facing away from him.

The Distractions of Others Can Be Dangerous

A side effect of family strife, God's family or otherwise, is that it can be distracting to the point that you make serious mistakes in your own life. Think of a young woman whose eagerness to leave a critical and dysfunctional family drives her into the arms of an abusive man. Think of a first-year college student who finally breaks free from a clinging and enmeshed family only to be enticed by new freedoms that result in bondage, and serve as distractions from pursuing the career of which he or she dreamed. Or what about you? Think about all of the time you can waste by focusing on the strife and chaos of others. It can be difficult if not disastrous to live your life when your mind is preoccupied with these distractions.

I almost painfully learned this lesson of not letting others distract me when my wife and I were driving home from church one Sunday. It began when we followed a man and his wife out of the church parking lot and turned onto a four-lane road. This had great potential for frustration because he always drove extremely slowly. Even though the road had two lanes in each direction, he seemed to think the dividing line between our two lanes was for centering his vehicle. When he inadvertently swerved and managed to get his entire car into the right lane I seized the opportunity and passed on the left. As I was increasing my distance from him, I watched in my rearview mirror as he corrected his error and re-centered his car on the line. Just as I thought, "I sure hope he doesn't cause an accident," my wife yelled, "Stop!!!" There was a *turn signal-less* parked car in front of me that had stopped abruptly for either a left turn or an insurance settlement. I barely made it into the right lane in time to avoid plowing into it. When I looked in my rearview mirror again, I noticed that my brother in Christ had finally found his way safely back into the right lane. He probably said to his wife, "Did you see Mills up there? That idiot's going to get somebody killed." My focusing on him almost did.

Questions

1) Do you find yourself continually focusing on someone else or family strife? If so, what are the consequences to you? Are you trying to win their approval or avoid their wrath? If so, whatever happened to the importance of your own approval of yourself and your own inner peace?

2) If you continually focus on others, is it because you do not believe you are worthy enough to focus on yourself? If so, who taught you that?

Disrupting Your Inner World

Everything in your outer world has a representation in the inner world of your mind. When I just wrote about my brother in Christ who took his half of our two lanes out of the middle, I did not go to his home and ask him to re-orchestrate the experience. No, I replayed it in my mind. I had my original outer experience in which I almost plowed into the car in front of me, and my inner representation of that experience as I recall it.

By thinking through the experience again for you, it has resulted in me becoming a bit irritated with him all over again. How could he be so inconsiderate? He's probably sitting at home judging me as I write this. I should have followed him home and given him a piece of my mind. That self-centered jerk doesn't care about me or my wife! Next Sunday I'm going to glare him down!! I'll show him. I'll leave church early so he can't control how I drive. That'll fix him!!!

Then again, he probably did not even see what happened. I am the one who is inserting what I think he thought and said. On second thought, as I continue to replay it over and over, he undoubtedly thought and said worse. In fact, he probably set me up!!!! He had to know what he was doing!!!!!

You might think I sound a bit foolish writing about someone this way, but you have probably done the same in your mind. You may even replay an event and embellish it again and again, and revise your recall until you are finally the *winner*. The problem is that if you do this, you end up losing *another day* trying to win a *previous day's battle*. In essence, your inner world becomes disengaged from your present, and it becomes even more dangerous to your mental, emotional, physical, and spiritual well-being than your current outer world.

If you are really committed to disrupting your inner world, the good news is that you are not limited to the past. You can imagine and meditate on an infinite number of happenings in the future with an unlimited number of endings. You can be the all-conquering hero or the eternal victim, whichever suits your psychological need or self-image. To paraphrase Mark Twain's quote with a substitution, "I am an old man and have known a great many [victories], but most of them never happened." Or if you prefer, "I am an old man and have known a great many [defeats], but most of them never happened." If you find yourself *replaying* unpleasant memories, try *re-praying* them instead.

Questions

1) Can you identify when you have allowed your inner world to become contaminated with fruitless worries and phantom battles?

2) In your inner world, are you the eternal victor or victim? What do you gain from either?

3) Are you pre-playing your future? If so, what are you looking for in your predicted outcomes? It is best to prepare for the future, and then trust the Holy Spirit when what happens, happens.

4) How can replaying and pre-playing be redeemed? Hint: Replay the past with forgiveness, and pre-play the future with trust.

Protecting Your Inner World

Ministering to others means being engaged in the outer world of *one mores* where true victories are achieved. As you take Jesus as your yoke and learn from Him, you will become a better steward of your mind, which will provide you with greater peace and allow you to minister more effectively. You can do this because in the Gospel of John Jesus says, "I have told you these things, so that in me you may have peace. In this world you will have trouble. But take heart! I have overcome the world" (John 16:33). Once again, Jesus promises that His followers will have trouble. Even so, He also says that He has overcome the world. The only thing that remains is for us to allow Him to overcome our inner world by continually presenting it to Him.

As I wrote previously, the Apostle Paul offered the Philippians some very practical guidance about worry, anxiety, and how to keep their inner world safe.

> 4 Rejoice in the Lord always. I will say it again: Rejoice!
> 5 Let your gentleness be evident to all. The Lord is near.
> 6 Do not be anxious about anything, but in every situation, by prayer and petition, with thanksgiving, present your requests to God. 7 And the peace of God, which transcends all understanding, will guard your hearts and your minds in Christ Jesus.

> 8 Finally, brothers and sisters, whatever is true, whatever is noble, whatever is right, whatever is pure, whatever is lovely, whatever is admirable—if anything is excellent or praiseworthy—think about such things. 9 Whatever you have learned or received or heard from me, or seen in me—put it into practice. And the God of peace will be with you. (Philippians 4:4-9)

Taking Jesus as your yoke and learning from Him is first about yielding your inner world to Him. In essence, you need to continually present your inner world as a living sacrifice, and remain as a branch in His vine. From this foundation you can reach out to others more effectively through the power of the Holy Spirit. This does not mean you will not get wounded from time to time or perhaps even mauled. It does mean, however, that you can heal and grow in your wisdom. It also means that you can become shrewd while remaining innocent, which will enable you to minister with conviction, understanding, and an inner peace.

Questions

1) Has being hurt by others shaped your inner world? If so, how?

2) How can you present your inner world as a living sacrifice?

3) If you could experience the presence of Jesus in your inner world, how might your inner battles be different?

4) Which wounds of your inner world have been healed, and how did your healing occur?

5) Do you still have inner wounds that need healing? If so, how might your healing occur? Would talking with someone help?

Be Authentic in Your Outer World

Another way to keep your inner world safe is to be as authentic in your outer world as possible. Let your *yes* be your *yes* and your *no* be your *no*. It is however just fine to not always say what you think, because you may not always think what you currently want to say. Remember, once something is said it is forever said, and cannot be unsaid or unremembered by the person to whom you said it, unless gracefully it is forgotten. There are those who claim, "I just tell it like it is." No, they tell it like they *think* it is. We have to wait for God to finally tell us all *what it was*.

Being authentic also does not mean always doing what you are free to do in Christ. The Apostle Paul wrote of this to the Corinthians in his first letter.

> [31] So whether you eat or drink or whatever you do, do it all for the glory of God. [32] Do not cause anyone to stumble, whether Jews, Greeks or the church of God — [33] even as I try to please everyone in every way. For I am not seeking my own good but the good of many, so that they may be saved. (1 Corinthians 10:31-33)

This means that you can be authentic and gracious, and you do not have to argue with everyone who does not share your view. You can be authentic and *speak silence* in love.

It is fine for us to conform to the needs of others as long as it does not deform us from the image of who we are in Christ. As with the Apostle Paul, we should know who we are on the inside while we are seeking "the good of many." This is not an inauthentic compromise, rather, it is wisdom that meets people where they are, and leads with love, not a lecture. We need to first show our love in order to earn the right to speak God's truth. Otherwise, our tongue may be nothing more than a reckless six-year-old child driving God's *Scripture-car*.

I recall a German Shepherd for whom my authenticity would not have been seeking his good or my own; he needed a rabies vaccination and he hated men. No problem because we had an excellent female veterinarian who would see him. Unfortunately, she woke up that morning to the one sick day of her employment, and my receptionist was not able to contact the dog's owner. When the owner arrived and was told of the situation, she said she could not reschedule because she had taken time off from work and would be leaving on vacation soon. To make matters worse, she said her dog would not tolerate a muzzle. I told my receptionist to tell her to go along with whatever I did.

Before entering the examination room, I took off my lab coat and tied it around my waist. From outside the door I called out, "Hellooooo?" in the highest-pitched voice I could muster. I came swishing in through the door like a female fashion model on a runway, and in the same voice said, "We're heeerrre for our examination and rabies vaccination todaaaayyyy. Pleeeeease hold his head." I completed the examination and gave the vaccination while the dog peacefully looked out into the hallway. Mind you that I had a beard at the time. The owner gave me a look and slowly shook her head from side to side as if to say, "I can't believe you just did that. No one will ever believe this. Good job, I think?" I thanked her and swished out of the examination room. That is when my inner little boy who tried to take credit for the *embedded-rubber-band-head-transplant* was left unsupervised for a moment too long and did something I'm still not particularly proud of. I stuck my head back in the room and said, "Good dog" in my normal voice. He immediately spun around and looked at me with rage in his eyes. I pulled my head back quickly with the panicked thought that I might have forgotten to do everything he needed. Upon rereading his medical record, to my relief and no doubt his, our relationship had successfully found closure.

I have no idea what other men had done to him, but he was exhibiting serious transference towards me. Both of us were fortunate that his rage towards men was so tightly stereotyped to a deep voice that he missed the beard completely. People can put up similar walls and aggression, and sometimes there is nothing you can do to gain their trust or bypass their defenses. You can only love them and make accommodation for their wounds until they feel safe enough to trust you and let Jesus into their inner world for healing. We must always remain true to who we are and do our best to present ourselves in a way that others can receive.

Questions

1) How have you struggled with conforming to the desires of others without deforming from who God wants you to be?

2) Identify a time when you conformed successfully to the desires of someone else without deforming? What did you do?

3) When it comes to being authentic, do you have the right to speak God's truth if you are not living God's truth? How does being an imperfect and forgiven person relate to speaking the truth in love?

Jesus Can Transform Your Wounds into Convictions

Being conformed to the image of Jesus is the result of many forces that can include our physical health, difficult circumstances, and difficult people. God is like the hands of a potter with one hand on the inside and the other on the outside to form the pot as it spins on the wheel. Sometimes forces on the outside are God-sent as the Apostle Paul believed about his "thorn," (2 Corinthians 12:7) or God-allowed. Even when God allows difficult circumstances or people to hurt us, He is faithful and we can say what Joseph said to his brothers who sold him into slavery, "You intended to harm me, but God intended it for good to accomplish what is now being done, the saving of many lives." (Genesis 50:20).

I do not believe Joseph's statement means that God "intends" sin. Rather, God redeems the sins and evil intentions of others, including our own, for His purposes. That said, just because an experience is excruciatingly painful does not mean that it could not have come directly from the will and hand of God. The crucifixion of Jesus comes to mind.

It does, however, seem easier for Joseph to say, "...God intended it for good..." when he has already been freed from his prison, though he no doubt fought hard during his confinement to keep his faith, and hold on to the promise he received from God in his dreams. It is much more difficult for a victim of child abuse, rape, or other violent crime who is still living in the shattered shards of his or her life to be optimistic that, "...God intended it for good to accomplish..." His will. Ultimately, we have to trust and wait until Jesus returns to know for sure what was redeemed and what was intended.

As horrific as life may be or has been for you, or whatever wounds and voids you carry, it is vital for you to remain in your vine and branch relationship with Jesus, and to continually present yourself as a living sacrifice by climbing with whatever strength you have back onto God's alter and onto His potter's wheel. Painful experiences can become either the clay for your convictions, or the justification for your bitterness and retreat. Either way, God loves you just as much if you are on His wheel or on the floor. He loves you just as much if you are a branch of His

Son's vine, or alone on the ground. While Jesus said that apart from Him you could do nothing, in His hands, you can become His hands to minister to those who also have been wounded in the same way you have. As I wrote previously, He always redeems what you offer.

Convictions into Ministry

Your wounds can heal into convictions that God uses to minister to others through you. If you were abandoned and had to heal alone, you can make sure someone else does not have to do the same. If you have learned wisdom, you can make sure someone else does not have to remain in confusion. If you were assaulted physically, mentally, emotionally, or spiritually, and are finally able to regain enough strength and healing to stand again, you can stand and guard someone else until they are able to stand as well. Then the two of you can find and help someone else to stand. Throughout all of your trials and disappointments, your ultimate hope can only be in a merciful and just God who uses your painful experiences to accomplish His will – perhaps even with the same result as Joseph's "saving of many lives."

To recap, when helping others, make sure what you are doing is truly helpful, and not just perpetuating their dependence on you. Acknowledge the fact that some people will take advantage of you, and when this happens, accept your newly acquired wisdom and grow forward. Listen to your discernment, and challenge your transference to see if it is laced with an inappropriate bias. Do your best to stay out of unhealthy relationship triangles, and if you find yourself in one, expose the truth immediately. Avoid gossip and protect your inner world at all cost. Be as authentic with others as you can, and do not allow yourself to be deformed to the patterns of this world. Above all, let Jesus heal your wounds and transform them into convictions.

Questions

1) Have any of your wounds been transformed into convictions that led to ministry? If so, which ones and how did it happen?

2) What wisdom have you learned from being wounded and then healed that you can pass on to a new believer?

3) Do you have wounds that are still robbing you of your *one mores*? If so, who might you reach out to for help?

CHAPTER 16
Well-Balanced Christians

It is easy to get so focused on the personal struggles of ourselves and others that we lose sight of how it would look and feel to be a mature well-balanced Christian. Not only must lies be revealed, challenged, and discarded, God's truth must to be added. Christians can best accomplish this demolition and construction when they are *well-balanced on God's altar* where He can renew their mind.

Becoming a well-balanced Christian is especially challenging for those who did not grow up with the better parents, families, or caregivers because it is difficult to imagine what has not been seen. What follows is a list of traits that characterize mature well-balanced Christians.

1) Mature well-balanced Christians understand who they are as individuals in God's eyes apart from their various roles in life. They are the same person when functioning as a parent, spouse, employee, employer, pastor, lay minister, or friend. When asked who they are or what they do, their answer is not confined to a single role.

2) Mature well-balanced Christians can authentically and freely experience a wide range of feelings such as joy, excitement, sadness, or anger without having a nagging inner critic tell them what they should or should not feel.

3) Mature well-balanced Christians can control and regulate their feelings such that joy does not skyrocket them into an uncontrollable euphoria, and sadness does not plunge them into

the depths of despair. When sadness or disappointment occur, well-balanced Christians prevent a disabling long-term emotional impact by grieving appropriately, praying, meditating on Scripture, and if necessary, seeking wise counsel from others such as a family member, pastor, friend, or therapist.

4) Mature well-balanced Christians believe they have a right to pursue and accomplish their own goals and desires without feeling the need to please or seek the approval of others. These "others" include family, friends, and the omniscient, omnipresent, and ever-elusive group known as "they." Many Christians are completely obsessed with what "they" might think or say. Various authors are credited with the idea that people would be far less concerned with what others thought of them, if they knew how seldom they did.

5) Mature well-balanced Christians believe they have a right to ask for and receive help without ridicule or condemnation, and are willing to do the same for others.

6) Mature well-balanced Christians have an appropriate sense of satisfaction and accomplishment when they achieve a goal or overcome a difficulty. They do not wear a yoke of false humility and self-deprecation. When you congratulate them for an accomplishment they can actually respond by simply saying, "Thank you."

7) Mature well-balanced Christians can relate to others empathetically without losing their own sense of individuality and autonomy. In essence, they can understand and care for others who may be experiencing a horrific tragedy, and still maintain a separate appreciation for their own life, along with its joy, sadness, and challenges.

8) Mature well-balanced Christians believe they not only have a right to their own preferences and opinions, but also have the option to defend them when confronted by others who would insist otherwise.

9) Mature well-balanced Christians can freely commit to a relationship with someone and regulate the depth of physical and

emotional intimacy to what is spiritually appropriate, and not be overly concerned about being rejected or abandoned by the other person.

10) Mature well-balanced Christians are able to identify and work at intentionally changing behaviors that are not desired, or are no longer helpful.

11) Mature well-balanced Christians can accept that they live in a fallen world, and they understand that despite the tragedies that occur, God is ultimately merciful and just.

To be honest, this list is pretty depressing to me because I am not that mature or well-balanced, and I do not know anyone who is. That acknowledged, maturity and balance for Christians begins and remains in their vine and branch relationship with Jesus as they continually present themselves as a living sacrifice to God for the renewing of their minds. Even with a vine and branch relationship, and presenting oneself to God regularly, becoming a fully mature Christian is a continuous process that cannot be finished during our earthly stay. It requires our faith that God can change us if we present ourselves to Him, and our trust that He will. We also must remember that sometimes His will is to do nothing, or as the Apostle Paul recounts in 2 Corinthians, intentionally do something that is painful.

> 7 ...Therefore, in order to keep me from becoming conceited, I was given a thorn in my flesh, a messenger of Satan, to torment me. 8 Three times I pleaded with the Lord to take it away from me. 9 But he said to me, "My grace is sufficient for you, for my power is made perfect in weakness." Therefore I will boast all the more gladly about my weaknesses, so that Christ's power may rest on me. 10 That is why, for Christ's sake, I delight in weaknesses, in insults, in hardships, in persecutions, in difficulties. For when I am weak, then I am strong. (2 Corinthians 12:7-10)

Paul points out that God is not solely preoccupied with our personal strength, and is primarily concerned with the strength of Christ in us. In the same way, we dare not become solely preoccupied with our own spiritual maturity because that is accomplished for us as we yield ourselves to the filling and flowing of the Holy Spirit, and learn how to discern and respond to His prompting. Our preoccupation needs to be with presenting and yielding ourselves to God, which will give rise to disciplines of grace such as reading Scripture, prayer, and fasting when able.

Just as a Club of christ can become preoccupied with reaching in, to and for itself, and fail to reach out to others, self-absorbed perfection-seeking Christians can do the same when following a regimented set of rules and behaviors. These Christians do not realize that their flesh can thrive when feasting on non-sensual delicacies such as self-sacrifice and commitment when done apart from the power of the Holy Spirit, which results in self-justification, self-glorification, and a pride-filled offering to God.

Paul was not congratulating the Thessalonians for being a successful group of Jesus impersonators when he wrote, "You became imitators of us and of the Lord, for you welcomed the message in the midst of severe suffering with the joy given by the Holy Spirit" (1 Thessalonians 1:6). What Paul acknowledged was their joy in the midst of their suffering, which was authentic and given by the Holy Spirit, and not a self-manufactured ecstatic bliss. Jesus also made it clear that he was not looking for a group of cloned impersonators when He said, "I am the vine; you are the branches. If you remain in me and I in you, you will bear much fruit; apart from me you can do nothing." (John 15:5). It is only by remaining in Jesus that we can imperfectly reach out to a world in need that will languish unnecessarily if we wait to see a perfect image of Jesus in us, or worse yet, wait to carve our own graven image of Jesus on us through ascetic self-absorbed rituals.

Questions

1) What does the phrase "disciplines of grace" mean to you?

2) It has been said in James Chapter 2 that faith without deeds is dead. How could deeds without faith be even deader?

3) What could be wrong with being an "imitator" of Jesus?

CHAPTER 17
Offering Wise Counsel

When I refer to offering wise counsel I mean one friend helping another to understand his or her thoughts and feelings more clearly in light of God's Word. I am not advocating that one person direct the life of another, or that a layperson practice psychotherapy without a license. There is a dilemma, however, in that just as God does not have enough *imperfect and wise parents* to keep the world populated, He also does not have enough *imperfect and wise and available licensed therapists* to help everyone who is in need. Most effective therapists I know have waiting lists of weeks to months. For this reason, and the fact that we are yoked together in Jesus, we all may be called upon from time to time to help one another.

A caution is in order. Please do not use this material to try to help someone who should be working with a trained and experienced therapist. Anyone who is suffering from mental illness or a severe personality disorder needs professional help and may also require medication. People who need help from a professional do not need a friend who is sincere and untrained. If you are at all concerned about someone you are trying to help, you should consult with a pastor, therapist, or other trained professional. Underestimating the seriousness of someone's mental health issues can result in disastrous consequences. If you think you may be getting in over your head with someone, you likely already are – get them the help they need!

An important indicator that someone needs professional help is if he or she expresses thoughts of harming himself or herself, or harming someone else. Once again, the best help you can offer is to contact a trained professional who can assess your friend's risk and notify the appropriate authorities if needed. If you are concerned that your friend might get angry if you contact someone, the question you need to ask yourself is, "Would I rather have an angry friend or a dead one?"

Neurotic to Psychotic

Some therapists assess clients along a continuum of neurotic to psychotic. People who are neurotic have a medically healthy functioning brain, but struggle with specific patterns of thinking such as compulsivity, perfectionism, or self-esteem issues. People who are psychotic on the other hand, do not have a medically healthy brain and may be delusional, paranoid, or even hear what sounds like voices telling them to commit destructive acts that may include harming others, or even harming themselves to the point of suicide. These people need professional help, and once again, the best you can do is help them find a competent therapist they can trust. Your role may be limited to that of a supportive friend as long as you are physically safe when you are with them.

The Need to be Needed

Anyone in a helping ministry should ask himself or herself, "Do I need to be needed?" It is fine to want to be needed, but unhealthy to need to be needed. Helping someone should not be about your needs. Recall my patient with the amputated leg and how after she fell I was always outside of her cage when she stepped out. Was that for her benefit? Of course not. She never really needed me in the first place. She needed to realize that her left front leg was no longer there, which she did in one step. I was in her way from then on because of my need to protect myself from further self-condemnation.

If you fall into the *need-to-be-needed trap*, your well-being will likely be linked to your friend's choices and outcome. If your friend continues to make poor choices, you may feel like a failure, and if your friend gets better, you may feel insignificant because your friend no longer needs your help.

Many people who need to be needed actually use these types of dependent relationships as substitutes for balanced friendships. The rationale is often that if others need them, they will not leave, which eases their own fears of abandonment and loneliness.

The need to be needed and fear of abandonment are often characteristic of *enmeshed parents* or *caregivers* who refuse to let their children develop a sense of competence and independence. They fail to realize that their relationship with their child should evolve away from dependency. God's design is for both the parent or caregiver and the child to mature into their new roles as each is conformed more and more to the image of Jesus. The stunted alternative is a parent who demands dependence from an adult child, and an adult child who refuses to become who God intended, or is made to feel guilty when he or she tries. These same principles of developing competence and independence apply when offering wise counsel to others. The goal is for them to become competent and independent of you.

Questions

1) What are the differences between *wanting to be needed* and *needing to be needed*?

2) Do you know people who *need to be needed*? What does that look like? If you are discussing this question in a group, do not name a specific person so as to avoid the risk of gossip.

3) Do you need to be needed? If so, why? In what ways might that leave you and those you are trying to help vulnerable?

Convincing

Providing wise counsel to a friend should never deteriorate into convincing. Have you ever been asked, "Do you know of a good marriage convincer?" Or heard someone say, "I have an appointment with my convincer today." If you find yourself slipping into convincing mode you are doing a disservice to your friend. Chances are your friend has already experienced a long line of convincers who have left him or her confused and unable to think clearly for himself or herself. If you insist on doing the same, you will either hinder your friend's personal growth by perpetuating his or her pattern of unhealthy dependence on others, or activate his or her continued resistance to your pressure. In addition, you may as well be wearing a sign that says,

> The successful outcome of your life
> depends upon
> you letting me be your God.

By the way, if you ever find yourself on the receiving end of an energetic convincer you need to decide if you want to present yourself as a living sacrifice to God, or as a dress-up doll to your convincer.

Questions

1) Do you know any convincers? How effective are they?

2) Are you a convincer? When have you tried to convince, and what was the result?

3) How often does convincing result in lasting change?

Ambivalence

Most if not all trained counselors, and everyone else for that matter, find themselves in convincing mode from time to time. This usually becomes apparent when they realize that the other person is stubbornly resisting what is *obviously* true. The next time this happens when you are trying to give wise counsel, try gradually shifting your position to one that is more closely aligned with that of the person you are trying to help, and often he or she will shift to a position that is closer to what you were originally advocating. I used to think these people were just being argumentative and stubborn, but more often than not what I was experiencing from them was their ambivalence.

Before receiving a Masters in Social Work, I thought ambivalence meant someone did not care about something either way. Actually, ambivalence means the opposite in that a person cares strongly both ways. That is why when you oppose one position, they defend it, and when you switch sides they defend the other. Most of the time it is not that they are trying to be difficult, it is their inner ambivalence surfacing between the two of you. You are experiencing outwardly with them, what they are struggling with inwardly. In essence, for them to feel faithful to their inner conflict, when you take one position, they are compelled to argue for the other, and vice versa. For example, if a friend is leaning towards divorce because of adultery and you support that position, they may say, "Yes, but what about forgiveness? Shouldn't I forgive?" Then when you start supporting forgiveness, your friend responds by talking more about the violation of trust and reasons for leaving the marriage.

When people are struggling with ambivalence, the best way to help is to ask gentle, non-condemning, non-condoning questions, and give them time to answer because they need to hear their own thoughts and answers, not be bombarded with what you think they should do. Your goal should be to bring their ambivalence out into the open so they can see it more clearly. You do this by asking questions about both sides, while being very careful not to get drawn into a debate or argument. For example, you can ask, "If you stay together, what challenges will you need to work through?" and "If you get divorced, what pain goes away?" and "What additional challenges will divorce pose?" If your friend directs his or her anger towards you, relax and sit tight. Anger directed *towards you* is not the same as anger directed *at you*. Sometimes the anger needs to be discharged before thinking can begin. And never answer the question, "What would you do?" because you cannot possibly know until it happens to you.

Questions

1) What types of ambivalence have you seen in others?

2) How might you respond compassionately to someone who is experiencing ambivalence?

3) What types of ambivalence have you experienced within yourself? What questions can you ask yourself?

Contrarians

Ambivalence does not explain the difficulty of interacting with contrarians who disagree or modify everything you say or feel. These people remind me of a father and son who always hunted ducks together. Beginning in childhood, the son never stopped trying to impress his father. One morning when the son drove them to the marsh in his pickup truck for a hunt, he parked and let his new dog out of the back. The dog immediately sat next to the son who said to his father, "Watch this!" He threw a stick out into the water and the dog ran out on top of the water, picked it up, and ran back to shore without getting wet. The son said, "So dad, what do you think about my new dog?" The father shook his head slowly in disgust and said, "Take me home. There is no way I'm going to be seen hunting with a dog that can't swim."

The identity of contrarians is based on their opposition to whatever someone else is advocating. Engaging them is futile because they are not encumbered by having to come up with an original thought of their own. All they need to do is disagree with whatever you say. Some contrarians do not even limit themselves to what you say, but rather, distort your position and then argue against their own fabrication.

Another tactic contrarians often use is to create an absurd contrast such as, "Church services must be carefully planned with no deviation because no one wants chaos." Really? Are there only two options? No deviation or chaos? What about an *orderly responsiveness* to the ongoing ministry of the Holy Spirit?

When you find yourself contending with a contrarian you must be alert and relentless in restating your position, and dragging him or her kicking and screaming back to the accuracy of what you said, not their distortion. This is hard work and necessary if you have any hope for a mutually healthy relationship based on truth and love, and not one based on your need to convince and their need to contend. On the other hand, you can just let them talk until you can think of an excuse to escape. The choice to invest your time, energy, and *one mores* is yours.

Questions

1) What experiences have you had with contrarians? What would you advise a new believer who is caught in similar situations?

2) Do you have contrarian tendencies? If so, do they get you what you want and serve you as effectively as you think they do?

3) What would it feel like to let go of the need to convince a contrarian of your positions, values, and perhaps way of life?

The Need for Approval Revisited

Just as it is hazardous for you to *need to be needed*, you are equally in peril if you need the approval of others. For example, if you happen to be like that duck hunting dog with some amazing abilities of your own, and you do not receive the approval from others that you desire and for that matter deserve, you have two choices. The first is to continue serving Jesus with your abilities, and let go of your need for the approval of others. The second is to conform to their desires and *swim like a regular dog*. If you do, it is likely they will still criticize you for your unnatural stroke. It is fine to want the approval of others, but not to need it.

Questions

1) Do you need approval from someone? If so, how do you feel when you do not receive it? Is it worth it? What can you do to break free of this bondage?

2) Can you imagine what it is like to try to win the approval of a contrarian? Perhaps your imagination is aided by experience. What strategies can you recommend to a new believer on how to break free of the need for a contrarian's approval?

CHAPTER 18

Change

Occasionally you hear reports of someone being delivered instantaneously from an addiction or a self-defeating behavior. For most of us, however, change is a gradual process. The main difficulty is that change by definition is a choice that goes against our current desires, and if the change was easy it would already have happened. The bottom line is that we ultimately do what we ultimately want to do despite our mixed feelings, intervening periods of regret, and perhaps even an aftermath of self-condemnation that can flourish into self-loathing.

Change begins with an awareness that a problem exists. The Holy Spirit initiates a prompting that often is consistent with the encouraging and possibly near-violent insistence of those around us. Though this awakening is usually the easiest part of change, people often respond with justifications, excuses, or they perhaps even fall back to a defense of denial with questions such as, "What? Who? Me? Are you nuts? What's your problem?"

Once we accept that change is desirable we still must decide to change, make a plan, implement the plan, and maintain our progress while adjusting the plan as needed. This change often begins with the early victories of mechanically responding differently to a temptation long enough to let genuine feelings follow that become part of our authentic renewal.

A plan for change often includes an *encourageability partner* who can walk through the change with us. I prefer the term *encourageability* over the more traditional *accountability* because the latter is a bit pessimistic and failure-based.

When change begins to occur, we always need to be on guard against our original desires when they return to press themselves back into our experience, and their fulfillment. Their return should not be surprising since a decision to change is often made shortly after those desires have entered into a temporarily satiated slumber. Many a diet has begun at the end of a satisfying meal.

I understand that some may object to the idea that change is a result of our decisions and actions, and claim that it is God who changes us. My question to them is, "If my change is *completely* up to God, why has He not already done so?" I think they miss Paul's point to the Philippians by not noticing the phrase, "continue to work out your salvation with fear and trembling."

> [12] Therefore, my dear friends, as you have always obeyed — not only in my presence, but now much more in my absence — continue to work out your salvation with fear and trembling, [13] for it is God who works in you to will and to act in order to fulfill his good purpose. (Philippians 2:12-13)

It appears that the process of God changing us also requires our intent for the change to occur and persist. Of course, I am talking about real change and not the "change" offered by many self-help programs that only teach people to *act* differently while *remaining unchanged* on the inside.

Questions

1) Identify ways you have changed with a clear intent to do so. What worked for you, and why?

2) What are some behaviors that you want to change and have been unable to do so? What could make the difference between your success and failure?

3) Do you have an encourageability partner? If not, is there someone you could ask to walk with you on your path?

Failure

Failure is an essential component of change. It isn't a matter of *if* we will fail, because we will – repeatedly. The main question is, "How do we respond to our failure?" For many people, failure results in a cacophony of self-condemning thoughts in a sadistic serenade. For these people an inner voice says, "You are a hopeless failure. You will never be any different." If that happens to you, your only *sufficient* response is, "His grace is *sufficient* for me." Failing does not mean we are failures; failing only confirms that we are still in the process of being conformed to the image of Jesus. Of course, those who fail repeatedly and claim it is never their fault have a much deeper character flaw than their persistence at failing.

If failure for you results in self-condemnation, your thoughts may sound similar to those of your parents, caregivers, or people from your past who criticized and condemned you. The phrases you hear may even be word-for-word excerpts from their earlier declarations. At times you may even feel their presence as though they were standing right next to you. In reality they are even closer; their image is standing right *in you* in your inner world.

Self-condemnation when we fail can actually betray a deeper issue of pride in that we assumed we could never fail in that way a first time, or again and again. To receive victory in your battle for change and in overcoming your failures, you must continually decide to not let the deceit-filled thoughts of self-condemnation and self-destruction that self-effort provides, kidnap you from the truth-filled life of forgiveness and restoration that Jesus offers.

One type of failure that is often overlooked is the *fear of success* along with the responsibility and accountability that success brings. One can justifiably be asked a similar question as what Jesus asked the disabled man at the pool, "Do you want to succeed?" For some, the honest answer is,

"No. I want you to feel sorry for me and take care of me. I also expect you to continue making excuses to others for me. Now, if you will excuse me, I need to finish this video game before I get to my social media."

Questions

1) What is your experience with self-condemning thoughts when you fail?

2) If you have self-condemning thoughts, do they sound like the words that others from your past have said to you? If so, who? Is it possible those people could have been wrong about you and were clueless about the future God has planned for you?

3) What would you tell a new believer, your best friend, or your child about how to handle failure or self-condemning thoughts?

4) Does your answer to question 3 also apply to you? If not, why?

5) Do you have a fear of success along with the responsibility and accountability that comes with it? If so, what is your fear costing you, those you could help, and those who love you?

Calvary or Mount Sinai

If self-condemning thoughts are so painful, what purpose do they serve, and why do we hold on to them? Roy and Revel Hession propose in their book, *We Would See Jesus*, that when we fail, Satan wants to drag us from our failure to Mount Sinai where we face condemnation from the law. The Holy Spirit, on the other hand, wants to carry us to the cross where we receive grace from Jesus.

We can either go to Mount Sinai and find death at its top, or lie down at the cross and receive life at its base. On the Mount we offer our flesh and sweat as a dead sacrifice to a dead law, while at the cross Jesus offers His flesh and blood as a living sacrifice to God's law. On the Mount we make our own whip and flog ourselves in search of our own regret and exoneration, whereas at the cross we repent and accept the blood of Jesus, and receive His mercy and forgiveness. On the Mount we flog ourselves in a disillusioned self-worship that on our own we should and could have done better. At the cross we present ourselves as a living sacrifice that knows it never was or ever will be good enough on its own.

Why would we choose self-condemnation and self-flogging at the Mount of the law over repentance at the cross? Self-condemnation and self-flogging at the Mount allows our self-edifying religious pride to avoid a personal crucifixion, and to continue in its belief that it can climb the Mount on its own terms, by its own effort, and step from the top of the Mount into heaven. It is only after receiving life from Jesus at His cross and the gift of the Holy Spirit that we are equipped to climb any mountain to which He calls us. We are either the dead climbing to satisfy ourselves through serving the law, or we are the living climbing to satisfy our Lord by serving Him and loving others. We were created to climb and what matters is where, for whom, and by whose power.

There is a third option other than Mount Sinai or Calvary, and that is a Sodom and Gomorrah where what is abhorrent to God is declared righteous. There are no furtive glances of impropriety, nor are there looks of concern. There is only an unrestrained and open brazenness of a mutual self-indulgence of the flesh, reinforced by one another's echoes of baseless affirmations. These affirmations eventually ring hollow in the emptiness of one's soul when they fail to provide true freedom and true rest.

Even when flesh and unbridled desires are allowed to reign, they cannot silence the whisper of the Holy Spirit calling the hearer to come to Calvary – the cross of Jesus. God's voice cannot be silenced by a hardened heart, and even when someone is given over to depravity, the Holy Spirit still speaks God's love. The arms of Jesus are always open for our repentance. In fact, it is for us that he allowed them to be nailed open.

Questions

1) Calvary, Mount Sinai, or Sodom and Gomorrah, where do you go when you fail, and why?

2) Why can grace be difficult to receive?

3) Is Sodom and Gomorrah only for those who struggle with gratification of the flesh, or is there also a neighborhood for those who worship success, and live for the gratification of their pride?

Gradual Transformation

It bears repeating that the type of change most of us experience is a gradual renewal of our minds to the point where a decision can be made and we have the commitment and resolve through the power of the Holy Spirit to make it permanent.

The promise of instant change makes for exciting preaching and can increase financial giving, but sadly, it often leaves its hearers disillusioned in a wake of unfulfilled hopes and expectations. As I wrote earlier about healing, preachers who promise instant change, will likely claim that any lack of change is due to the hearer's lack of faith. God will always honor checks for promises He writes on His account, but will not do so for frauds who claim His name in vain.

Change is challenging because once we become aware of behaviors or thoughts that are no longer wanted, they are already a heavy yoke that has embedded itself into our neck. In addition, we have to overcome a certain numbness that enabled us to tolerate its presence. These wounds from the past, protective defenses, and personal agendas left unchallenged, continually seek deeper and deeper places of agonizing comfort in us. That is why continually presenting ourselves as a living sacrifice and abiding in Jesus are essential for discovering and dislodging their strangulating grip. To meet this challenge, I cannot overstate the importance of an *encourageability* partner and a healthy congregation to help you navigate your renewal.

Change is a Response

Change is a response to wearing Jesus as our only yoke, learning from Him, and responding to the Holy Spirit and fellow believers. This change is possible and lasting when we enter into and remain in our vine and branch relationship with Him, and our branch and branch relationships with other Christians.

Change is also a response to God's grace that offers new hope, new desires, and new ways of thinking. The behaviors that previously made sense at some level, despite their destructive outcomes and long-term consequences, no longer make sense based on new desires. Where walls were desired and built for mental and emotional protection, relationships are now desired and built for mental and emotional fulfillment. Where anger was desired and used to repel and defend against others, love is now desired and used to embrace and serve others. Where bitterness was a salt that painfully preserved the wounds of the past, forgiveness is a salve that allows them to heal.

Change is an Action

A "changed" mind based solely on new insight without an accompanying change in behavior is like faith without deeds. It is all too easy to get caught up in the narcotic mist of insight alone. In fact, the exhilaration of new insight can even be a rewarding psychological defense against acknowledging and experiencing real brokenness, repentance, and change. Those who are content with only a change in their thinking without a change in their behavior should not be surprised when others who are in relationship with them are not so similarly satisfied.

Personal Change Benefits Everyone in the Body of Christ

Ultimately, Godly change in us is our being conformed more and more to the image of Jesus so we can have a deeper experience of belonging in His body, and be better able to love and serve others. Christians are like individual pieces of a puzzle that are continually being shaped to become a better and better fit with one another in His body. As we are gradually and individually conformed more and more to His image, we become more and more equally and uniquely yoked together in Him to become His image of grace and mercy to a watching and waiting world. This is why it is so important that we encourage one another by speaking the truth in love, and by providing wise counsel through the guidance of the Holy Spirit.

Barriers to Change

There are many barriers to change. For example, believers who struggle with drugs, alcohol, or addictions to food or pornography know these behaviors ultimately cause pain, anxiety, and anguish to themselves and their loved ones. Even so, while these behaviors are being acted out they bring some sort of relief and satisfaction. As such, they can be difficult to let go of because they often serve as anesthetics that treat an even greater inner pain. For this reason, there is often a strong and very real benefit to not changing because when these behaviors are stopped, the addicted are more often than not left alone with the same original pain that drove them to their addiction in the first place. It is very difficult to substitute a sweet poison that initially causes the pain to cease, yet results in destruction, with a new behavior that initially allows the pain to remain, yet promises peace.

Discovering and healing our deeper wounds can be a long and arduous journey through dark memories. Healing may even require a competent counselor and fellow *survivors and thrivers* who have experienced similar wounds, darkness, and despair, and have endured the pain of fighting back to wholeness. Part of their healing and victory, more often than not, includes helping others who are on a similar path.

It is important to remember that change is a gradual process of being conformed to the image of Jesus, and it takes longer than a lifetime. If you are ever frustrated with your lack of progress, I ask you to give yourself only as much grace as you would to a young child, or your best friend; no more and certainly no less.

Questions

1) Do you have barriers to changing a behavior? If so, what are they?

2) What benefits do you receive from not changing?

3) If you are struggling to change a behavior, who can you find to walk this path with you?

Barriers to Change in Relationships

A barrier to change when it comes to relationships is that some people do not want to change when they are already getting most of what they want when they want it. They are quite content with the status quo even though the other person in the relationship is giving far more than he or she intended, and receiving far less than anticipated. For example, a friend may frequently ask you for favors or help, yet be consistently unavailable when you are in need. If you confront him or her about the one-sided nature of your relationship, he or she may become offended, and may even try to use projection to convince you that you are the one who is being selfish. Even so, you may still choose to give of yourself with the full acceptance of their lack of a mutual response. However, if you do, make sure your giving is intentional, and that their lack of response does not give rise to a root of bitterness in you.

One-sided relationships are particularly endemic with Christian abusive husbands whose entire *Own Testament* consists of a single corrupted verse,

> "Wives, submit yourselves to your husbands. The wife does not have authority over her own body, but yields it to her husband. Do not deprive each other. And if she divorces her husband and marries another man, she commits adultery." (All About Me:1:1)

I know how much my father-in-law loved his daughter, and that was nothing compared to how much God loves her. Picture a husband who has died and is standing before Jesus as he gives an account of his life. The first thing the husband says to Jesus is,

> "I really want to thank you for those verses requiring my wife to have sex with me, and not allowing her to divorce me. If it wasn't for them, I wouldn't have had any sex, and she would have left me long ago. A marriage based on the Bible is wonderful."

Now, imagine Jesus' response,

> "Yes, I'm glad you mentioned your wife. Do you

remember that she is my sister and my Father's precious daughter whom He knit together in her mother's womb? She and I met in prayer daily and she often spoke about how you treated her. You cannot imagine how pleased I am to discuss this with you face to face.

"How dare you eat fruit from her garden in which you refused to plant, cultivate, and nurture? How dare you demand her *services* without *serving* her in the same way I serve you? You took and did not give. How dare you turn my Words of life to her into chords of bondage from you? I agree with you that a marriage based on the Bible is wonderful, but do not speak of something with which you have no experience."

Questions

1) What one-sided relationships have you been a part of, and which side were you on?

2) Have you ever confronted someone who was taking advantage of you? How did that person respond? Was confronting them difficult? If so, why? What was at stake?

3) Is there someone now who is taking advantage of you that you need to confront? Why haven't you? Do you need other believers to help you? Ideally, your goal for confrontation should be to build a more meaningful and God-honoring relationship.

CHAPTER 19

How to Give Wise Counsel

This chapter is *not* about *what* counsel to give a friend because that depends on the specific situation, and is between you, your friend, and the Holy Spirit. Rather, it is about the *process* of giving wise counsel, and how to understand yourself and your friend while doing so. This chapter also exposes common traps to avoid.

One-on-one counseling is a three person process in which you should listen to the Holy Spirit; your own thoughts, emotions, and physical reactions; and those of your friend. It is imperative that you never lose sight of the fact that every person you counsel is unique, and the relationship between the two of you will be unique. Even if you have endured the same trauma or have suffered under similar circumstances, their personal experiences, ways of persevering, and path of healing will not be the same as yours. This does not mean, however, that the wisdom you have learned from your experiences will not be helpful to them.

Answers Are Not the Answer

Wise counsel is not a set of prepackaged canned answers, cookbook recipes, or intellectualized quick-fix-slap-a-verse solutions. These types of "solutions" are only valuable in that they may ease the anxiety of the one offering counsel who feels obligated to always have an "answer" for someone's problems. Another reason for offering these "solutions" can be that the one offering counsel simply feels uncomfortable being present with another person who is struggling with strong emotions, and sees a quick "answer" as a way to end his or her own discomfort.

When helping others, you should not see yourself as a mechanic to whom people bring their mental or spiritual car to be "fixed." Rather, your role is to help them discover and understand themselves in a way that allows them to work towards healing and growth in partnership with the Holy Spirit. Otherwise, they will keep coming to you for answers, which aborts their own journey of spiritual growth. Then again, if you need to be needed, having an "answer" for everyone's problems may be an addiction to which you are compelled, not a mission to which you are called.

If "answers" are not the answer then what is? Studies have shown that when various types of counseling are compared, the main predictor of therapeutic success for clients is how they perceive the quality of their relationship with their therapist. As such, people generally heal best in the presence of a safe, non-judgmental, non-condemning, and trusting relationship in which the truth is spoken in love with compassion under the guidance of the Holy Spirit. This does not mean, however, that the relationship does not have boundaries, accountability, and if necessary, biblical confrontation.

If our relationships with one another are so important for healing, think about how important a relationship with Jesus is for those who turn to you for help. As brilliant and effective as you may be, you must never lose sight of their need to turn from seeing you face to face, to seeing Him face to face. It is fine for you to initially be their source of truth, hope, and encouragement, but your purpose should be nothing less than to wean them from a necessary and temporary dependence on you, to an independent relationship with Him. Your ultimate goal for those you are trying to help should be for them to develop the ability to seek wisdom and hear the Holy Spirit for themselves, and to thrive in their own personal vine and branch relationship with Jesus.

One final thought: If you are consistently working harder than the person you are trying to help, there is a problem. Your role is to *walk with*, not get out ahead and pull someone to where you think he or she should go.

Questions

1) Are you an answer giver? If so, how can you be more helpful?

2) What does it mean to provide a safe, non-judgmental, non-condemning, and non-condoning presence while someone thinks through his or her issues?

3) How often do people respond well to condemnation?

4) Can you recall times when you were consistently working harder than someone you were trying to help? If so, what could you have done differently?

Boundaries

Counseling a friend is often about boundaries, and many times there has been a long history of boundary violations that have resulted in mental, emotional, physical, or spiritual harm. It is also possible that the person you are helping has violated the boundaries of others. Either way, it is important that you model a healthy relationship by setting and defending if necessary your own boundaries. This means giving only the time and energy that you intend to give so you do not feel abused. In essence, boundaries are about keeping your inner world safe, which is no small challenge when you regularly engage in the chaotic lives of others. If you ever find yourself wondering if you are giving enough, you probably have already given too much.

Questions

1) List examples of unhealthy boundaries that you have experienced or seen in others. Serving as someone's mindfill is an example. How can healthy boundaries be set and maintained?

2) Is it difficult for you set and maintain healthy boundaries with others? If so, why?

3) In what ways did Jesus maintain healthy boundaries?

4) What wisdom can you offer a new believer on how to establish, reestablish, or maintain healthy boundaries with others?

Do Not Forget Your Own Needs

It is difficult to hear the Holy Spirit for others and give wise counsel when you are so exhausted that you can barely hear Him for yourself. This does not mean that the Holy Spirit cannot use you when you are exhausted, but exhaustion should not be your *typical* state. Our best example of someone tending to His own needs and taking time for rest and prayer is Jesus who "…often withdrew to lonely places and prayed" (Luke 5:16). And if His example is not compelling enough, even a dog with a litter of puppies knows enough to get up, shake them off when necessary, get some food and water, and take a needed stroll in the backyard. And how those puppies (and people) will howl. I'm not exactly sure what they say, but it probably falls along the lines of, "How could you leave us?" "We're all going to die!" "You are selfish and don't care about us!" Or, "You are only thinking of yourself!" At first these accusations and demands may cause the dog (or you) concern, but eventually she learns that everything will be fine as long as she takes care of herself enough to have something to give.

If you have friends or church members like those puppies who become a constant drain on your energy, and you will, I hope you are at least as smart as that dog who also is smart enough not to wander the neighborhood nursing all of the other puppies, only to come home and find her own puppies weak and near death, or worse, having been visited by a hawk. And why would anyone fall into this trap? Perhaps it is the result of trying to win the approval of others and live up to their expectations. There may also be a need to be needed. It may even be due to an incorrect view of God that sees Him as a nearly impossible to please tyrant who demands such a performance before accepting anyone into His presence and giving them His approval.

In Matthew 16:26 Jesus asked the questions, " [26] What good will it be for someone to gain the whole world, yet forfeit their soul? Or what can anyone give in exchange for their soul?" A similar pair of questions could be, " What good will it be for someone to minister to families of the whole world, yet lose their own? Or what can anyone give in exchange for their family?"

Questions

1) Have you invested enough time and rest in yourself to maintain a sustainable and effective ministry? Do you have a plan for continuing to do so?

2) How have you dealt with people who demand more from you than you are willing and called by God to give? What would you tell a new believer about how to respond to those who demand more than he or she is willing to give?

3) Have you spent too much time in the "neighborhood nursing all of the other puppies" and not enough time at home? Remember, hawks are always watching your puppies. Do you need to make changes?

Do You Want to Get Well?

As we discussed in previous chapters, when counseling a friend, you should always ask yourself if he or she really wants to get well, or perhaps is only using his or her circumstances to get and keep your attention. This may sound cynical, but once again this question is one that Jesus asked. Let's read this passage from the Book of John again.

> 5 ¹ Some time later, Jesus went up to Jerusalem for one of the Jewish festivals. ² Now there is in Jerusalem near the Sheep Gate a pool, which in Aramaic is called Bethesda and which is surrounded by five covered colonnades. ³ Here a great number of disabled people used to lie — the blind, the lame, the paralyzed.⁵ One who was there had been an invalid for thirty-eight years. ⁶ When Jesus saw him lying there and learned that he had been in this condition for a long time, he asked him, "Do you want to get well?"
>
> ⁷ "Sir," the invalid replied, "I have no one to help me into the pool when the water is stirred. While I am trying to get in, someone else goes down ahead of me."
>
> ⁸ Then Jesus said to him, "Get up! Pick up your mat and walk." ⁹ At once the man was cured; he picked up his mat and walked. (John 5:1-9)

This passage does not mean that everyone gets well who wants to, and those who do not get well did not want to enough. However, it does raise the question about what someone really wants. Does he or she really want to regain personal control and take responsibility for his or her own life, or is there only a desire to get attention and be nurtured by others?

Many a counselor has fallen into the trap of nursing full-grown adult puppies who did not want to get well and walk on their own. If you do, you are colluding with the forces that originally took them captive by allowing them to build a new dependence on you. In addition, you may also become captive to their cravings for nurture to the point that they will not be satisfied until you place your mat next to theirs. Ultimately, nursing others who should be feeding themselves will make you ineffective for God, and is even less rewarding than my friend's experience working in a doughnut shop in New York City to which God did not send her.

Questions

1) Is there anyone in your life you should ask the question, "Do you want to get well?" If so, in what ways can you be more effective in helping them?

2) If someone you are trying to help is struggling with regaining control and taking responsibility for his or her life, could it be that others are better trained than you to address his or her needs? If so, whose help could you encourage that person to get in addition to having you as a friend?

Sometimes People Just Need a Little Encouragement

The story of the man at the pool reminds me of an elderly Golden Retriever that a client brought to me one day for euthanasia. She could barely hold back her tears when she said she thought it was time to "put him down." She said he refused to eat and could not get up. My staff used a gurney to transfer him from her van into the examination room and they put him on the floor so he would be more comfortable.

I knew this dog well and had been caring for him for many years. The first thing I noticed was that mentally he was *still in the room* because his eyes followed me at times and he knew what was going on around him. While he was laying there, I offered him a treat that he quickly swallowed and looked for another. He also did not have that tired *far-off* stare in his eyes that animals often get when the end is near. I knew his time was coming, but it was not today.

I walked to the exit door of the examination room, spoke his name, placed my hand on the door knob and said, "Get up and walk." He immediately struggled to his feet and stood there looking at me to make the next move. I opened the door and he looked back at his owner as if to say, "Are you coming?" My client looked relieved and somewhat embarrassed. I said, "Today is not the day." She followed him as he walked slowly out of the room, past the reception desk, and into the waiting room. He waited patiently at the door for her to take him out to the van. It is amazing what dogs and people can do when they are encouraged by someone who speaks the truth in love. Besides, there is nothing more motivating for a dog to walk than a chance to leave a veterinarian's examination room.

Two weeks later, it was the day. He had the *far-off* stare and was unconcerned about who was in the room. He was tired and ready. For most veterinarians, robbing disease of its final suffering by bringing a merciful and fitting end to a wonderful relationship between a pet and its owner is a great privilege and an honorably sad endeavor. It takes wisdom to know when the battle against disease is over, and the battle against suffering begins.

Sadly, the price clients pay for having a great pet is the grief they must endure when it dies. The only remaining comfort is their fond memories. This unavoidable grief is also true of our relationships with loved ones. For this reason, work for peace with them, a true and lasting peace based on speaking the truth in love, and setting boundaries without building walls. Strive to share as many pleasant *one mores* with them as you can because there will come a time when it is no longer possible.

When a family member dies, few people make comments such as, "Life is short, we should have argued more. There are so many hurtful things that I just didn't have time to say." Even if you think someone is a wholly unredeemable instrument of evil, let their evil remain with them. And do not let bitterness remain in you because it is their stench, and it will end up robbing you of your *one mores*. I have heard it said that holding on to bitterness about someone is like eating rat poison and expecting the rats to die.

Questions

1) Are there people in your life towards whom you hold bitterness? If so, is reconciliation possible? If it is, how can you do so, or at the very least, let go of your bitterness and trust God to settle the matter?

2) Are there people who are not alive that you still hold bitterness towards? If so, how can you create a resolution? It is safe to say that if they have repented and are in heaven, they would immediately make restitution with you if it were possible. And if they are not in heaven, nothing bitter you can think about them will add to their misery.

Questions to Help Friends Understand Themselves

As I mentioned previously, helping friends who want to change something in their life can be frustrating if you fall into convincing mode. What is more effective is to help them look at themselves and their situation in a genuinely curious and non-condemning way. What follows are some questions you can ask to help a friend become more observing and thoughtful about himself or herself and a behavior that he or she is trying to change.

Could you take a moment or so and look at yourself with love and not condemnation?

If your best friend was struggling with this, would you condemn or offer encouragement?

What encouragement would you offer?

What would change look like to you?

What would change feel like to you?

Have you ever wondered why this behavior is so difficult to change?

How does your current behavior help you?

What anxiety does your current behavior soothe?

What anxiety does your current behavior create?

What anxieties do you have about changing this behavior?

Do you really need this behavior anymore?

Is this behavior getting in the way of something you want more?

Is this behavior serving you in the same way you originally thought it would or needed it to?

What could life look and feel like if you would present this behavior to God as part of your living sacrifice?

Remember, it is important when asking your friend a question to wait for an answer. Even if your friend does not know the answer, it is fine for him or her to sit in silence and think. Try to remain accepting without condoning or condemning. If your friend starts condemning himself or herself, you may be tempted to respond by offering a rebuttal or encouragement. If you do, it is likely that you are only choosing one of his or her ambivalent positions and stepping into the trap of reenacting his or her inner conflict. A better response might be, "If what you are saying is true, what does that mean?" Or, "How might you look at this differently if this happened to your child or best friend? "

The main purpose of your questions is to help others look at themselves from a more observing perspective so they can see themselves more clearly based on their answers. Your questions serve to bring their thoughts into the open, so they can hopefully better understand what they are thinking and feeling. The goal for you is to help others see their behavior in light of God's truth and grace, not your opinions. That is why it is important for you to be patient and not be afraid to give the Holy Spirit time to work through you. Let Him use your authentic loving relationship to model God's character and heart.

A non-condemning non-condoning stance does not mean that God's truth is watered down. Rather, it means that His truth is not used to psychologically beat someone into a false and temporary repentance. It is much easier to hear the loving and perhaps convicting voice of the Holy Spirit when the condemnation of self and others has ceased. By the way, a side benefit of helping others look at themselves in a non-condemning non-condoning way is that you, hopefully, will also learn to do the same for yourself.

Questions

1) How often has someone's condemnation of another person brought about a desire in that person to have a relationship with Jesus? *Loving* someone to Jesus is much more difficult, and much more effective than *condemning* someone to Him.

2) How often have you heard a nonbeliever say about a Christian or a congregation, "Even though we disagreed about my lifestyle and personal choices, I always felt their genuine love for me?" I wonder how many people said that about Jesus.

CHAPTER 20

Pitfalls to Avoid When Helping Others

Helping others is not without risk. You must continually be alert and listen to the voice of the Holy Spirit and your own intuition.

Vicarious Trauma

When providing counsel, beware of vicarious trauma, which occurs when you feel traumatized just by hearing what someone has endured. I will again paraphrase Mark Twain's quote with a different substitution, " I am an old [counselor] and have known a great many troubles, but most of them never happened [to me]." It is difficult to have empathy and still maintain a healthy mental and emotional distance from the difficult and sometimes horrific circumstances of someone you care about. You may even find yourself becoming weary because you are trying to carry your friend's burdens.

There is a misconception that if we *carry the burdens* of others that it somehow lessens their load. This is rarely true. The burdens that we end up carrying are often our own self-manufactured duplicates of theirs, which does not lighten their original load at all – though they may feel less abandoned and alone, which can lessen the additional burden and pain of feeling alone. For example, we cannot make someone's adult child repent and follow Jesus, or bring someone's spouse back to life, but we can make sure they do not have to carry the additional burden of being alone while they are struggling with these trials.

To be even more direct, carrying the duplicated burdens of others is not being the hands and arms of Jesus working in the power of the Holy Spirit. Rather, it is well-intentioned flesh headed for *religious martyrdom*. If martyrdom is not bad enough, the real tragedy is that your friends are not receiving the help they need. There also is the danger that Satan can bring you down through his attacks on them. Think about it. Even if you could carry the actual burdens of others, how many burdens or partial burdens could you carry in addition to your own? Would your solution be to find your own friend to help you carry your ever multiplying load?

So what can you do to avoid what has been referred to in the secular literature as *compassion fatigue*? You can do what Jesus needs you to do, so He can do what only He can do. Jesus needs you to stand with your friend and intercede with prayer. Jesus needs you to listen for guidance from the Holy Spirit as you model the trust you want your friend to experience in his or her own relationship with Him. Jesus needs you to support and walk with your friend, while He and the Holy Spirit offer and provide when accepted, the necessary grace and inner strength for your friend to carry his or her load. It is from Jesus, through your love and prayer and presence that your friend will receive God's provision and strength to carry his or her burdens.

Questions

1) What are your thoughts on carrying the burdens of others? In Galatians the Apostle Paul writes, "Carry each other's burdens, and in this way you will fulfill the law of Christ" (Galatians 6:2). He also writes in the same Chapter, "Each one should test their own actions. Then they can take pride in themselves alone, without comparing themselves to someone else, [5] for each one should carry their own load" (Galatians 6:4-5). How do these verses relate to the idea that Christians often fall into the trap of carrying the self-manufactured duplicate burdens of others.

2) Does it make sense to distinguish between helping someone bear up under his or her burden, and your efforts to carry the burden for them? If it does or does not, why?

Vicarious Vengeance

When offering counsel to others it is important to be as unbiased as possible. For example, if a woman who has been abused by men is offering counsel to a friend who is having problems with her husband, she needs to keep any of her own unresolved wounds and emotions regarding men to herself. For example, she may say to her friend, "You ought to leave that ungrateful fool because he will use you up and walk away without giving you a second thought." While it is possible that the husband of the woman receiving counsel will *use her up and walk away*, the advice of the previously abused woman is nothing more than her acting out her own vengeance towards men.

On the other hand, a woman who has survived an abusive relationship and fought to heal her wounds is likely to be much more qualified to help other women. She, unlike *Randi the pigeon*, was able to escape from her hawk and learn wisdom from the experience. She understands that even though her own abusive relationship was unique – snakes, hawks, and wolves share many characteristic patterns of abuse and manipulation. Much of what is learned from encountering one snake, hawk, or wolf is true about the others.

Questions

1) Have you experienced times when someone's "wisdom" was more like vicarious vengeance? If so, what did you notice that helped you make that determination?

2) Can anyone, including me, offer you unbiased wisdom? How can choosing verses from the Bible or other writings for you to read indicate someone's bias?

Dislike at First Sight

Since this chapter is about pitfalls to avoid when helping others, I think it is helpful to revisit *subconscious transference*. If you are in a helping ministry long enough, you will eventually be asked to help someone you immediately dislike and have no idea why. This can be disconcerting with a tendency to *confess your sin* and try to move forward without regard for your feelings. Please do not ignore this source of insight about your thoughts, emotions, and possibly unresolved wounds that were triggered by this person. As I wrote in Chapter 15, Relationships can be Painful, ask yourself what therapists are trained to ask themselves: "When have I felt this way before?" "Are there others from my past or present who trigger me to have similar feelings and react this way?" It is often helpful to share these feelings with a wise friend, and present yourself along with your unsettling feelings to God as a living sacrifice. When you do, the Holy Spirit will lead you in how to respond. You may even be unable to minister to that person until you work through some issues of your own. There is no *spiritual crime* in this because we all are imperfect people who are in the *process* of being conformed to the image of Jesus. That said, if you must continue to interact with this person, I was taught in my social work training to find and focus on at least one positive character trait, and trust God to work things out from there as you continue to respond to His insight and leading.

Questions

1) Are there types of people you dislike? What are their traits? Which of their traits are similar to your own? If any, is it possible you are projecting your dissatisfaction with yourself onto them?

2) Are any of the traits you described above characteristic of people with whom you have had difficulties in the past, such as parents, caregivers, or peers? Do you have wounds that need to be presented to God; possibly with the help of a friend or counselor?

3) Have you been disliked for being similar to someone else? If so, how can you be respectful and non-threatening, while not deforming yourself away from the image of Jesus.

Conviction From God or Condemnation

Before providing counsel to a friend, seek the guidance of the Holy Spirit and listen to your discernment. If you hear a voice telling you how bad of a person you are or how guilty you will feel if you do not do something, that is not the Holy Spirit. The Holy Spirit is encouraging, compelling, and convicting, not condemning. Would it not be hypocritical of God to sacrifice His Son to pay for the guilt of our sin, and then use guilt to control us? He leaves that kind of control to self-serving leaders. My point is, if you feel guilt and condemnation, it is not God. If you feel empathy and conviction, it probably is.

Questions

1) What role does guilt and condemnation play in your life?

2) Do you think God uses guilt to motivate us? Do other people use guilt to motivate you? How can our enemy or others use guilt to disable us?

Forces

Forces in a Helping Relationship

When trying to help someone, there are many psychological forces in the room. One force you should not overlook is that of a person you are trying to help, responding by trying to change you. Remaining in a helping relationship with someone like this can make life very difficult if you also want to be conformed to the image of Jesus. In essence, this is the same as trying to serve two masters. Jesus said,

> "No one can serve two masters. Either you will hate the one and love the other, or you will be devoted to the one and despise the other. You cannot serve both God and money." (Matthew 6:24)

Jesus could just as appropriately substituted money with mother, father, husband, wife, children, members of a Club of christ, friend, or anyone or anything else. It is clear that Jesus only wants you to serve Him and to be conformed to His image, not the images of others. He loves to give, but He does not like to share.

Another force to be aware of is that some people take pleasure in the *game of counseling* with the goal of refusing to change, while maintaining a pleasant facade of desiring otherwise. The joy for them is having someone else's undivided attention besides their own. A word of caution: If you happen to break through their carefully constructed barrier and touch an inner wound, you will likely be met with anger and condescension until they regain the composure of their defenses and resume playing the game. They may even try to make you feel bad for "hurting them."

Another force to avoid is your own desire to please someone you are trying to help in order to win their appreciation and approval. Left unchecked, this desire will cause you to continuously adjust and conform what you say based on their responses until you receive what you desire. You are to present yourself to God for appreciation and approval, not to others.

Perhaps the most devastating force to be on guard against when helping others is that of seduction, which usually begins without anyone's intent. Conversation and healing between two people who have wounds, empathy, childhood and adulthood agendas, and the prideful attitude that seduction could never happen to them, are key ingredients for creating an atmosphere of intimacy that attracts Satan like a moth to light. That is why if you are not a trained and licensed counselor, it is not a good idea for you to be in a helping relationship with someone of the gender to which you are attracted. However, if you must, do so with the direct involvement of leaders in your congregation who will keep everyone accountable to the hope and truth we have in Jesus.

If you do not take this warning about the force of seduction seriously, you need to understand that Satan is watching you like Randi the pigeon was being watched by the hawk. Randi was blessed in that she died quickly; you on the other hand will have to live with the destruction. Everything you care about will either be destroyed or forever distorted. Even with forgiveness and restoration, what is done can never be *not* done. I have witnessed God rebuild families who were nearly destroyed by seduction, and while they love each other and are grateful to Him, to a person they wish it had never happened.

Questions

1) When you help others, do you ever try to conform them into an image you want for them?

2) Have others tried to conform you into an image they wanted for you?

3) Are you serving multiple masters? If so, who or what are they? Are these "masters" external people or your own internal gods, goals, or agendas? How can you bring these multiple masters back under the Lordship of Jesus? Hint: Presenting yourself as a living sacrifice has something to do with it.

4) Did you take my warning about seduction seriously? If not, as I said, Satan is watching you like Randi was being watched by the hawk – unless you are the hawk. This is why the entire congregation needs to continually be on guard for predators, both inside and out.

CHAPTER 21

Helping Others Can Be Painful

One morning a woman and her young daughter arrived at my hospital with a shoebox that contained a fledgling cardinal that had all of his feathers, but was not yet able to fly. His tiny body was limp, showing no signs of life. I gently removed him from the box and cupped him in my left hand with his body resting in my palm. With my thumb on the same hand I began stroking him gently, beginning at his head and slowly moving down onto his back. Much to my relief he opened his eyes. Relief can be fleeting.

As it turned out, this semi-comatose barely-clinging-to-life beauty of nature was only sound asleep. When I awaken in the morning I am fortunate that I can take my time and have a cup of coffee before I interact with others. This poor defenseless little guy did not have that luxury. He opened his eyes and there was my face, about a foot from his own. A millisecond later he saw my thumb poised for yet another caressing stroke. That is when he must have seen my swollen and infected hangnail. That itty, bitty buzzard bit down right in the middle of the red, raised, succulent tissue and he liked the taste. I could tell because he did not shake my thumb and spit it out like the Cocker Spaniel. He closed his eyes tight in savory bliss and spread his tiny wings straight out from his sides. He obviously was too young to have received the memo that veterinarians were always trying to help.

As the pain became nearly unbearable due to his tin snipping beak and my preexisting infection, the thought occurred to me that he must feel trapped so I lowered my hand to the table allowing him to slide out onto the surface. His eyes remained shut, his wings remained extended, and he still did not let go. I slid my hand down the table away from him. He remained attached and followed like a glider being towed by another plane down a runway for takeoff. Oh how I wanted this tiny glider to let go because it was all I could do to keep my pain reflexes from swinging my arm to freedom, which would have cause him to be launched like a rocket. I finally convinced my reflexes that the rocket option would not work out well for me or my license to practice veterinary medicine, not to mention the years of psychotherapy for my new client and her daughter.

When Jesus talked about giving, He said that one hand should not know what the other was doing. Not so when a single thumb is up against the demonic and now catatonic beak of destruction. My right hand immediately flew into air support and hovered over its stricken brother wanting to help, but having no idea what to do. It could not figure out how to non-lethally pry open the clamped beak of this baby bird. We had all kinds of safety equipment at the hospital, but no one thought to order a miniature jaws of life that could be used to free me from these miniature jaws of death.

When my knees started to get weak as though they thought the solution was on the floor, my right hand's first mission was to steady my swaying frame by grasping the edge of the table. As my knees regained some of their strength, my right hand let go of the table, dropped below the surface, and offered me a suggestion.

The suggestion began with its thumb reaching forward and placing itself squarely on the nail of the middle finger. The thumb then pulled back until the finger was curled and taut with the other three fingers in straight extension. It assured me that it could deliver an ever-so-gentle flick that would dislodge the gargoyle's grasp. All my rescue hand wanted from me was a green light to emerge from below the table and my torture would be over in an instant.

Of course, I knew as well-intentioned and persuasive as my thoughtful right hand's plan was, the only outcome would have been the little birdie's bodiless head taking off on his first flight – with my detached thumb fixed firmly in his beak. No, with the weakness returning to my knees, it was better to pass out on my floor than tap out on his head. About then he must have opened his eyes and seen my helpless submission and impending fall because he let go and folded his wings neatly back along his sides. I would like to think it was due to his mercy, or even his personal satisfaction from his victory over the giant. Not likely. He probably just did not want to be pulled over the edge of the table, even though he would have landed softly on my limp body.

Relief can fleet back in the release of a beak. I looked up and both mother and daughter were staring at me in anticipation of my diagnosis. They seemed oblivious to the near-death struggle that had just played out in front of them. They may even have thought this was my sophisticated test of the little guy's neuromuscular system. I took a deep breath and said, "I think he's fine. It is best to return him to where you found him because I am sure his mother is worried." If she was, she was needlessly so.

There will be people who come into your life like that baby cardinal who at first seem to obviously need your wise counsel. Unfortunately, they may not be aware of their *obvious* need and your *obvious* qualifications. They already know what they want when they want it, and will find your *obviously infected hangnail* if you do not comply. They have no interest in talking about a better path, or being told that if they keep doing what they are doing, they will keep getting the same results or worse. This means that if there ever was a time for you to be *as shrewd as snakes and quicker than a baby cardinal*, it is when you are helping people.

Questions

1) Do you have wounds such as my infected hangnail that can be exploited by others? If so, what can you do for your healing?

2) How have you been *intentionally* or *unintentionally* hurt when helping people? What wisdom have you learned?

Knowing Your Vulnerabilities and Changing the Rules

Sometimes being as shrewd as a snake means changing the rules of how you are willing to be treated. While that baby cardinal probably just got lucky in latching on to my infected hangnail, people who are close to us can make our life especially painful and difficult because they know our vulnerabilities. The closer these people are to us, the more pain they can cause.

Unilaterally changing the rules of a helping relationship means that you do not have to keep offering your thumb as a living sacrifice to the mouths of Cocker Spaniels and beaks of baby Cardinals. Of course, in order for you to change the rules you must first believe you have the right to be treated differently. This can be difficult because your *new rules* are likely to be at odds with your childhood training or they would not be *new*. As mentioned previously, we initially look to parents, caregivers, and peers to tell us what is right or wrong, acceptable or unacceptable, who we are, and how we should be treated. Unfortunately, looking to them for truth can be like looking into a distorted mirror; the reflected image is more characteristic of their disturbed inner world than our reality.

Changing the rules often requires putting on the full armor of God and believing you have a right to be who God says you are rather than who others may have trained you to think you are. Changing our beliefs and putting on God's armor is usually a gradual process that begins with an awakening that the status quo is no longer acceptable. As such, it is fine to be discerning of where you are in the process, and to protect your vulnerabilities from further assault. That is what I had to do next with that calloused cardinal that was now resting comfortably on my examination table in his quiescent innocence.

After I proclaimed him to be healthy, I was faced with the problem of getting him back into the shoebox. I certainly was not going to let my hangnail get anywhere near him again, and my right hand was deep in my pants pocket not willing to volunteer its services having seen what the left had just gone through. Tilting the box onto its side and using a broom crossed my mind, but I knew that just wouldn't look right.

I finally decided to scoop him up using both palms, with my fingers folded completely and safely backwards laying flat on the back of each hand. I will be the first to admit that it looked a bit clumsy, and that is what it will feel like for you when you begin changing the rules about how you are willing to be treated, and how you are willing to interact with those you are trying to help.

Of course, the more you are conformed to the image of Jesus and the more you change the rules about how you are willing to be treated, the more likely you are to be treated to the same rejection and persecution He was. That said, the point of your Christian journey is for you to be conformed by God to His desired image for you, not for others to conform you to their desired image for themselves.

Questions

1) Are you in a helping relationship in which you want to change the rules on how you are treated? If so, what are your options? What would change look like in your interactions?

2) When is it appropriate for you to be abused in a helping relationship?

3) What wisdom would you offer someone in a helping relationship who wants to change the rules on how he or she is being treated?

When Helpers Need Help, Friends Are Not Mind Readers

I still am not done with that *thumb-carving* cardinal. My client and her daughter did not lift a finger to help me, which makes sense given the agony they saw my thumb going through. They obviously did not need a sign in my waiting room telling them who the veterinarian was. But then again, maybe they did not know about my pain because I tried my best not to show it. My point is that sometimes your life is difficult and others do not help because they do not know how much you are hurting.

Then again, there is no guarantee that pastors, family, or friends will help when you express a need. This may be because they are already overcommitted, do not know how to help, or perhaps are fearful of becoming overwhelmed. If that happens to you, find a qualified counselor. Remember, caring for your physical, mental, emotional, and spiritual health is your responsibility. You need to have the courage to put yourself first by setting, and defending if necessary, your boundaries with others. One boundary that is difficult for some people to overcome is that of their own pride or fear that keeps them from getting the help they need from a counselor. It takes courage to reach out for help.

If you seek counseling, it is critical that you find someone with whom you can build a trusting relationship, and this will take time. It is also important that you do not conceal your pain, and that you be as honest as you can about your feelings because feelings are not "right" or "wrong," they just are what they are at the moment. Exploring these feelings and thoughts with a qualified counselor can bring insight and unlock many of the reasons you do what you do.

Counseling in its highest form is a journey with someone you trust who is always an advocate for who God intends you to be. If you choose a counselor and you are not making progress, there is nothing wrong with finding someone else. Most counselors will even help you with your search to find someone who is a better fit for you because they are first and foremost concerned with your needs, not their own ego or income.

Questions

1) Do you expect others to read your mind and know your needs? If so, why? Did others from your past expect you to read theirs?

2) Do you have difficulty expressing your needs to others? If so, why? Are you trying to avoid disappointment if they fail to respond?

3) What reservations if any would you have about going on a mental, emotional, and spiritual journey with a trusted counselor?

Judging Others

Even though people are not mind readers, they often judge others based on a sovereign certainty as to what others are thinking. Ironically, someone's judgments about the attitudes and motives of another person can be more revealing of his or her own because we often see people more as we are, not as they are.

Consider someone making the statement, "She thinks she's better than everyone else because she won't even acknowledge who else is in the room." The reality may be that the person making the accusation does not acknowledge others who are thought to be inferior, and is projecting that attitude onto the woman. Or, the person making the accusation may have a fragile ego and needs affirmation from others in order to feel less insecure and accepted. When she does not receive the affirmation she wants, she harshly judges the woman for withholding. It is also possible that the woman who does not acknowledge others is dreadfully shy and on the verge of having a panic attack. Her ability to even leave her home may be the result of years of successful psychotherapy for having been abused as a child. Then again, she may be arrogant and condescending. My point is that it is very difficult to know what is happening in the minds of others unless they tell you, and even then you cannot be sure. A word of caution, self-proclaimed mind readers do not like having their lack of mind reading ability pointed out to them because they *know* exactly what your motives are for doing so.

Questions

1) How often do you hold court and sit in judgment of others? If you do, what joy or relief does it give you?

2) How do you think Jesus would respond if He found you sitting on His judgment seat?

Cast Outs and Outcasts

Some people have no desire to change, and they will leverage their wounds and your willingness to help for their own personal gain. It goes back to you asking them the question, "Do you want to get well?" Their honest answer may be, "No, that is too much work. I really just want your time and attention." Colluding with their unwillingness to be conformed to the image of Jesus is not being the arms and hands of Jesus. It may be necessary for them to experience the consequences of their choices, and for you to offer your *one mores* to others who really need and want them.

A friend once told me about a mutual acquaintance, and how terrible it was that the guy was pushed away by people and that he seemed to be, "abandoned in the corner." I was familiar with several years of this person's background and replied, "Spiders aren't pushed away, they crawl into corners to spin their webs." This person had taken advantage of several people from various churches and was not truly in need. Jesus was much more direct when He said, "Do not give dogs what is sacred; do not throw your pearls to pigs. If you do, they may trample them under their feet, and turn and tear you to pieces" (Matthew 7:6).

That said, if a pig ends up wearing one of your pearl necklaces, learn from it, accept the increase in your shrewdness, make more pearls, and get back to serving God by ministering to others.

Questions

1) Which pigs have ended up wearing your pearls and how did they manage to get them?

2) What wisdom have you learned about those who take advantage of others that you wish you had known when you were a new believer? Would you have listened?

3) Has anyone taken advantage of you in a way that limited or forced you out of ministry? If so, is God calling you back to serve in a different way? If you did return, what would you change?

CHAPTER 22

Cages and Hovering

Stay Out of Their Cage

As I wrote previously, Ratso, our rat-cobra, made it very clear that he did not want anyone in his cage at any time for any reason. Our oldest daughter who was about ten years old at the time received a nip on her finger to prove it. Interestingly enough, we never had to remind her to stay out of his cage again because she quickly became *as shrewd as a Ratso*. Even though he refused to change, her change was immediate and long lasting.

Some people want you to climb into their cage, and once you do, you can easily fall under their control and end up with a lot worse than a nipped finger. They want you to be the one who finally gives them what they want when they want it – all of the time. For others, their "cage" may even be a carefully spun web in the corner. As I wrote before, the thought of healing their wounds does not even occur to them because their wounds are part of a strategy for enticing others to take care of them.

One strand of their web might sound like, "Without you I have no meaning or purpose in my life." Or "You are the only reason I keep on living. I would die without you." Really? Aren't those the kinds of statements that should be said to Jesus? If you were in a relationship with this person and you died unexpectedly, do you really think he or she would stop breathing? A far more likely occurrence is when you leave the relationship because you are depleted and have nothing more to give, they will find another web-servant in the same way they found you.

It is not healthy for you to let others conform you to the image of *their* Jesus, and to convince you to provide for them what He Himself will not, which is to continually give them what they want when they want it. Once in their web it can be very difficult to get out. But then again, some people who appear trapped in someone's web, actually like being a Jesus impersonator along with the notion that someone needs them. They do not consider their need to be needed a trap at all. In fact, if you try to liberate them, you will likely encounter considerable resistance and be rebuked for your harsh insensitivity and lack of empathy for their web-king.

Questions

1) Has anyone tried to entice you into their web? Were they successful? If so, what was it like?

2) What wisdom can you offer new believers on how to identify and avoid people who try to trap them in their web?

Cages Can Serve a Purpose

Cages are not necessarily undesirable for those who live in them. Our youngest daughter had two gerbils that lived in an aquarium. They had plenty of food and water, a steady supply of toilet paper tubes, and the obligatory exercise wheel. The rules of the cage seemed clear. Certain areas were made for sleeping, the tubes were made for chewing, and the wheel was made for running – and that they did. And for those who feel bad for gerbils in cages, my daughter also had a cat who would regularly face-plant on the aquarium glass. My point is that people often live in cages of their own creation and have their own set of cage rules to make them feel safe. Anyone who is allowed to enter their cage must play the cage games by their rules.

If someone is asking for help, it is wise to stay out of their cage and make sure they really want to get well. If so, bid them to come out of their cage just as Jesus did with Lazarus.

38 Jesus, once more deeply moved, came to the tomb. It was a cave with a stone laid across the entrance. 39 "Take away the stone," he said.

"But, Lord," said Martha, the sister of the dead man, "by this time there is a bad odor, for he has been there four days."

40 Then Jesus said, "Did I not tell you that if you believe, you will see the glory of God?"

41 So they took away the stone. Then Jesus looked up and said, "Father, I thank you that you have heard me. 42 I knew that you always hear me, but I said this for the benefit of the people standing here, that they may believe that you sent me."

43 When he had said this, Jesus called in a loud voice, "Lazarus, come out!" 44 The dead man came out, his hands and feet wrapped with strips of linen, and a cloth around his face.

Jesus said to them, "Take off the grave clothes and let him go." (John 11:38-44)

It is fine to stand at someone's cage door and bid them to come out, but be very careful if you go in because inside their cage you may become trapped in the same near death experience of their life. Once people decide they want to be well, and are willing to come out of their cage into a life of freedom, the Holy Spirit is free to work through you to release them from any "grave clothes" that continue to bind them to their past.

A Cage Built Around a Cage

When people are willing to emerge from their own cage or one that was imposed on them through circumstances and perhaps poor choices, others who have built outer cages around them should, with discernment, be willing to remove those bars as well. This reminds me of a pair of ferrets we owned named Nippy and Muddy. We eventually had to build them a four foot by four foot cage with walls of chicken wire, and we placed a cardboard box inside for them to sleep in. When we put them in the cardboard box for the first time, Nippy ran straight out through the door of the box and over to a corner of the cage and started scratching to dig out. Muddy stayed inside the box, and we could hear him scratching to find freedom as well. Eventually, he emerged from the box by its door and looked around a bit confused. If he had continued digging through the cardboard box and had emerged into the cage only to discover the chicken wire, one can imagine his initial elation followed by disappointment.

In the same way, it is disheartening for someone to finally respond to the calling of the Holy Spirit and escape from his or her cage only to be confronted by someone else's walls of "chicken wire." That is why discernment from the Holy Spirit and evidence of change are necessary when deciding how and when to restore someone to fellowship. Wishful thinking and words are cheap unless they are used to deceive; then they can become very expensive to you and your congregation. In Nippy and Muddy's case, however, we were unwilling to remove the chicken wire because we did not believe they had changed their conviction about using our carpet as a litter box.

People often build cages of prejudice and condemnation

around others in order to feel superior, and to prevent them from expressing who God created them to be. For example, in an effort to appear smart, someone may build a cage of stupidity around you. In an effort to appear successful and confident, someone may build a cage of failure and self-doubt around you. In an effort to feel righteous, someone may build a cage of shame around you using bars made of their own disowned and projected shame. They may even name you "Ratso" when in reality you are a "Millski" whose rage is due to years of neglect, deprivation, abandonment, and perhaps even torment. And why would you or anyone else accept being placed in one of these cages? More often than not, it is the price of belonging. In essence, the message is,

> "If you want to be a part of this family or remain in relationship with me, you will not be as smart and competent as I am, and you will believe that you are a shameful failure and fundamentally bad. If I am unhappy, it is your fault."

What gives these cages of prejudice and condemnation their strength is the respect and honor we give them. We can choose to fight the bars of others directly, which only strengthens them. Or, we are free to walk through the bars at any time once we place our acceptance, worthiness, and belonging in Jesus, and not in those who would hold us captive. Their bars of criticism and judgment built around us only matter if they matter to us.

Whether you are a gentle Millski, an angry Ratso, or somewhere in between, Jesus wants all of you, and the Holy Spirit wants to flow through all of you. So when you present yourself as a living sacrifice, bring your intelligence and your ignorance, your competence and your incompetence, your successes and your failures, your goodness and your not-so-goodness, your belief and your unbelief, and do not forget to bring your cage, and any cages that others have built around you. Recall Nathanael's question about Jesus in John 1:46, "Nazareth! Can anything good come from there?" With God, anything good can come from anywhere, especially you when Jesus calls you to "come out" of your cage and into His renewing love.

Questions

1) Have you built a cage to protect yourself? If so, is it accomplishing what you hoped it would?

2) Have others built cages around you? If so, what kind?

3) Who does Jesus say you are?

Out of One Cage and Into Another

Of course people who genuinely seek healing can faithfully step out of their cage door and into the door of a predator's cage, which includes self-serving leaders. That is why ongoing spiritual discernment by all members of the body of Christ and effective church discipline are so critical. Outcasts can be brought into a congregation, and predators must be identified, disciplined, and cast out if they choose not to repent and submit to the authority of the leaders. After all, Peter was told to tend and feed the sheep and lambs, not placate wolves and feed their pups.

Hovering

Staying out of the webs and cages of others is a somewhat limited black or white metaphor. The question is often not to stay in or out, but rather, how to remain at a safe mental, emotional, spiritual, and functional distance that does not overwhelm and suck you into someone's control and dysfunction. For these situations with people you are trying to help, family, other believers, or even people with whom you work, the concept of *hovering* may be more helpful.

Hovering means that you stay close enough to interact, but not so close that you lose your mental and emotional balance. You continuously monitor your thoughts and emotions, and create mental and emotional distance as necessary. My wife became especially good at hovering her finger over Ratso as she gently gave him the minimal amount of tenderness he was willing to receive. As much as she did not want "the look" of his impending attack to appear in his eyes, when it did she honored it for the warning it was and moved her finger to safety. Leaving her finger to be gnawed upon would not have been wise, nor would it have changed his world view. Even so, his aggression did not prevent her from offering what little kindness she could *safely* offer.

The real challenge when hovering is that it takes a tremendous amount of energy because the mental and emotional forces that you are balancing against are always strong and shifting. You must remain continually alert not to fall into familiar and frustrating patterns of thoughts, feelings, and reactions. In essence, recognize "the look" in others when it appears, and move your mind and emotions to a safer distance.

Questions

1) Do you have someone in your life with whom you have to hover in order to not be drawn into their chaos and aggression? If so, what are their behaviors and "looks" of warning? How do you react when you are getting drawn in too close?

2) How can a friend or spouse help you hover when you are visiting a loved one's cage? What strategies can you use?

You and Your Friend's Needs in a Helping Relationship

Knowing that you need to stay out of your friends' cages and that hovering may be required, what do you and your friends need in a helping relationship? The following two descriptions of what your friends need and what you need will sound very similar because helpers and those receiving help have very similar needs.

Your friends need you to remain at a wise mental and emotional distance. They need you to trust the Holy Spirit to begin and complete a good work in them. They need you to allow them to walk away if they choose because that is what Jesus allowed. They need you to pray and allow time for the Holy Spirit to work. They need you to believe they will eventually respond to God when they are ready. If a friend decides to pull back from the relationship, and then reconsiders and wants to return, your friend needs you to receive him or her with love and acceptance. Your friends need you to model a healthy curiosity about them in an effort to help them become more observing and non-judgmentally curious about themselves. Your friends do not need you to talk continuously and tell them what to think, feel, and do, and they do not need you to need to be needed.

Remember the ox cart? Your friends do not need you to drive their carts for them. Rather, they need you to *help them* figure out their own life and how to drive their own carts based on their own vine and branch relationship with Jesus. Failing this, you run the risk of your friends pursuing you rather than Him.

So what do you need in a relationship when you are helping friends? You need to remain at a wise mental and emotional distance. John wrote about this when Jesus was at the Passover Festival in Jerusalem.

> But Jesus would not entrust himself to them, for he knew all people. 25He did not need any testimony about mankind, for he knew what was in each person. (John 2:24-25)

There is a crucial difference between appropriately trusting people and entrusting yourself to them. Let's continue with your needs and your trust.

You need to trust the Father, Son, and Holy Spirit to begin and complete a good work in your friends. You need to allow your friends to walk away if they choose, because once again, that is what Jesus did. You need to pray and allow time for the Holy Spirit to work. You need to believe your friends will respond to God when they are ready. You need to willingly let friends pull back from the relationship if they want, and receive them back with love and acceptance when they are ready to return. You need to have and model a healthy curiosity about your friends, and help them become more observing and curious about themselves. You need to ask meaningful questions and let your friends do most of the talking so they can discover what they think and feel about themselves and the challenges they are facing. Once again, what you need in a helping relationship and what your friends need is very similar.

What We All Need as the Body of Jesus

We all need to be discerning and shrewd and innocent warriors who are fully prepared for the spiritual battles and difficulties that we encounter on our path. We all need to continually present ourselves as a living sacrifice to God so our minds can be renewed as we are conformed more and more to the image of Jesus. We all need wisdom and insight and stillness so we can hear the leading of the Holy Spirit. We all need a family of believers who love, accept, and encourage us to continue growing in our likeness to the image of Jesus and in our relationships with one another. We all need to wear Jesus as our only yoke in the same way the disciples did, and receive the same grace and rest for our souls they received. We all need each other.

Questions

1) What are your personal needs when it comes to a helping relationship, both in helping and being helped?

2) Describe healthy helping relationships that you have seen or been a part of.

"Today is Ours."

*We are born into a difficult world of deceiving lies, and redeemed into
Jesus' body of renewing love.*

Jesus begins each day with you by saying, "Today is ours." That
acknowledged, your mind and your time are yours to direct as
you choose. It is your life to invest in treasures in heaven or on the
earth. Each day is yours to intentionally live your life with Him
until for you, it is your final day and your temple is closed. On
that day, what has not been done will never be done by you.
There will be no more *one mores*, and no more opportunities for
you to make a difference in someone's life.

The good news is that today is not that day for you, and you
have many more *one mores* to give. Begin each day by presenting
yourself as you are on God's altar as a living sacrifice. Bring
everything to Him, especially your belief and your unbelief.

Rest from your striving and take Jesus as your only yoke so
you can learn from Him. Place your imperfect life and strength
into His perfect hands to be broken as He chooses into who He
wants you to be. He is easy and His burden is light. When you
find yourself weary, look for additional yokes that are hiding on
your neck, or perhaps have already grown into it. And when you
find them, present them to Jesus for Him to remove.

Seek the guidance of the Holy Spirit continually and surround
yourself with friends you trust who can speak truth into your life.
Grow into Jesus' body of believers to become His living feet, arms,
and hands going to and reaching out to a wounded and hurting
world. Let yourself be renewed as you are used to renew others.

Jesus in you is your hope for purpose, peace, and life, and the world's hope for salvation, comfort, and healing. Living your life in your unique vine and branch relationship with Him will be difficult and worth it. Living your life in Him and allowing Him to live His life through you is responding to your own Matthew Chapter 10 calling.

May God bless you on your journey of being conformed to the image of Jesus, and may you remain in His rest as you come to Him each day and take Him as your only yoke.

Continuing Your Journey

I am honored and blessed that you have invested your time in reading this book. I hope the Holy Spirit has used it to deepen your understanding of God's truth, and to bring about in you a more intimate oneness with Jesus, others, and yourself. I also hope you will continually present yourself to God as a living sacrifice because according to Paul, "this is your true and proper worship." Remember to follow *kneeling at the altar praying,* with *laying on the altar presenting.*

For the rest of today and every day after, seize as many opportunities as you can to give someone another *one more.* Continue to be the feet, arms, and hands of Jesus to those in need in your congregation, your local community, and wherever God sends you. You matter, and the difference you can make in the lives of others matters.

www.ingramcontent.com/pod-product-compliance
Lightning Source LLC
Chambersburg PA
CBHW061007280326
41935CB00009B/869